CW01020251

HUNGER

Read when hungry.

Terry Durack

HUNGER
TERRY DURACK

A Sue Hines Book
Allen & Unwin

My thanks to Ruth Metzstein and Michael Bateman of the *Independent on Sunday*, where most of these stories first appeared, for their own particular hunger for my writing.

First published in 2000

A Sue Hines Book
Allen & Unwin Pty Ltd
9 Atchison Street
St Leonards NSW 2065
Australia
Phone: (61 2) 8425 0100
Fax: (61 2) 9906 2218
Email: frontdesk@allen-unwin.com.au
Web: http://www.allen-unwin.com.au

National Library of Australia
Cataloguing-in-Publication entry:

Durack, Terry.
Hunger.

ISBN 1 86508 348 8.

1. Food—Anecdotes. 2. Cookery—Anecdotes.
3. Gastronomy—Anecdotes. 4. Food—Humor.
5. Cookery—Humor. 6. Gastronomy—Humor. I. Title.

641.013

Designed by Cheryl Collins
Typeset by J & M Typesetting
Author photo by Jason Loucas
Printed by Australian Print Group

10 9 8 7 6 5 4 3 2 1

contents

■ power & ritual

■ culture & conduct

■ Hunger

I once stole a piece of salami from an ashtray in a laundromat. It was one of those grey metal shoebox ashtrays that sat on the floor, against the wall. There, at the bottom, was a half-eaten length of thin, semi-dried sausage known variously as kabanos, cabanossi or kabana. Technically, I may not have been stealing, but it certainly felt as if I was. I was young, broke, and living away from home—not that there was a home to go home to. In other words I couldn't really afford my two-pack-a-day smoking habit, so I did without a few unnecessary luxuries. Food was one of them.

While I wasn't hungry in the extreme clinical sense of the word, I was hungry in an uncomfortable, empty, nagging, demanding, draining sense most of the time.

I had been brought up by a mother who was a very proficient and enthusiastic cook, and later by a gourmand 'uncle', who left me his almost belligerent, doting love of flavour. Food had always been a priority, a source of pleasure and of companionship.

Yet during this comparatively brief, ever-hungry period of my life food completely lost its allure. Unlike the cliché of the shipwrecked sailor, I had no fantasies of giant sizzling steaks, tubs of creamy mash, or bowls of baby peas dripping with butter. It was too dangerous to give food such control over my mind. I stripped food of its supremacy, reduced its appeal, and blanked out any traces of lingering aromas or spiced scents. Deliberately, I blurred the differences between sweet, sour, hot, and salty until they melted into a homogenous, anonymous blob. Otherwise I might have gone a little mad.

How do you describe hunger to someone who has only ever skipped lunch? It's like describing colour to the blind, or sex to a child. The doomed hero of Knut Hamsun's classic 1890 novel, *Hunger*, makes a fair stab at it:

> I noticed that every time I went hungry for quite a long time it was as though my brain trickled quietly out of my head leaving me empty. My head grew light and absent. I could no longer feel its weight on my shoulders, and I had the impression that my eyes showed too wide a stare when I looked at somebody.

The food lover's favourite scientist, Harold McGee, tells us hunger is an innate biological drive. Although we may think of it as being isolated in a single organ, this is not the case, the stomach movements we associate with hunger being only a secondary signal. The first triggers of hunger involve a delicate balance among nutrient levels in the blood, digestive hormones and a range of substances active in the nervous system. The different parts of the mechanism are galvanised, coordinated and finally translated into signals to the conscious mind. Mmm, hunger. Must eat something.

McGee succeeds in reducing hunger to the same sort of sensible, amorphous blob to which I reduced food. These days, I *like* to feel hungry, because I know that I will soon be fed. In that sense, hunger is anticipation, a fantasy about to be resolved. A little hunger is also called appetite, and it is this appetite that lends the food we eat a piquancy, depth, complexity and level of fulfilment that no relish, pickle, or condiment could ever hope to equal.

In spite of my guilt, that piece of salami should have tasted heavenly. It didn't. By the time I had washed it, cut off the chewed end, and sliced it into little uniform pieces, it was merely fuel. Something I had to do, had to eat, something medicinal that would take away the pain.

I chewed impatiently, without any pleasure, wanting it gone, swallowed and forgotten. I loathed myself more than I have ever loathed anyone before or since.

Ironically, I now lead a life dedicated to eating, cooking, drinking, and writing about it. I push food as if it were a drug. I glorify it, I glamorise it, I am driven by it. I want to eat more, learn more, taste more, and write more about food than anyone else, ever.

One hunger has replaced another.

anticipation & desire

"The dining table is our level playing field. We are at our most revealing, sensitive and intimate when something flat, hard and wooden lies between us and our loved ones."

■
Eating out:
a love story

There are some people who are really happy only when they're on a boat. On dry land, they walk with an awkward, compensatory roll, and squint into a distant horizon even when there isn't one. But put them on a sloop, ketch or clipper, and the transformation is immediate and graceful. Suddenly those funny-looking moccasins make sense, as their wearer lands like a cat on the deck, as confident and self-righteous as a Mormon on a doorstep.

I'm exactly the same—with restaurants. They're my beat, my stage, my village. I'm only truly at ease when wedged into an upholstered carver or perched on a bistro chair, my elbow resting on cloth or stainless steel. My music is the clink of cutlery, the ping of crystal glasses, the eeeek of a cork being pulled from glass, the native drums and cymbals echoing from the kitchen.

I revel in the anticipation, the curiosity, the company,

the hospitality, the dialogue, and the ongoing silent contract between those who dine and those who feed them.

The best time of all is that small window that occurs once you have settled in to the table, and have taken a moment to observe the nature of your surroundings. A tinkly drink is placed in front of you, and your order is speeding its way back to the kitchen. You're in the system. Food is imminent, and yet there is time to ponder the day and relish the present. This is the defining moment of dining, when all is well with the world; all is anticipation and joy.

Those of us who love the dining-out process relax into it like a bubble bath. We are members of the club, the community, the industry, the very nation of Diningland.

We can read a restaurant the way a lion sniffs the desert wind. Without even knowing it, we can pick up the tension in a waiter's stance, register a contradictory sound from the bar, or know from a hint of yesterday's oil in the air not to order the fish.

At table — our rightful home — we can do no wrong. We may stumble upon arrival and stagger out later, but put a crisp cloth before us and we are Baryshnikov. We can be as diplomatic as Blair, as manipulative as Hussein, and as romantic as a beardless, blue-eyed, Hollywood heart throb. The dining table is our level playing field when negotiating business or romance. In fact, we are at our most revealing, sensitive and intimate when something flat, hard and wooden lies between us and our loved ones.

It follows that, before long, we start to think that we

could run our own restaurant. Don't. I did, and ended up in hospital. My casual job as kitchen hand—never, *ever* start at the bottom—had me opening twenty dozen oysters on my first day. Until that time, I had only ever opened two dozen at a time, maybe three if anyone else wanted any. Somehow, a sliver of shell worked under the skin of my palm. Within two weeks, it had grown into something that resembled a giant pearl. My doctor looked terrified and told me there was nothing to worry about as he drove me to hospital.

Convalescing, I decided to stick to what I'm good at—eating in restaurants. I've trained all my life for it. I've covered the ground, done the research: Chinese, Lebanese, Indian, Japanese, Hungarian, Moroccan. New and old. Scary and comforting. Cheerfully cheap and breathtakingly expensive.

Never once have I become jaded, tired or cynical. I thrill to the chase of a fine new restaurant, and love to plug into the restorative power of an old favourite.

Restaurant: from the verb *restaurer*, to restore. That's what the good ones do. Put back what the day takes out. Add to your life what you didn't know was missing. Make you the person you always thought you could be. If only for two-and-a-half hours.

"It was what we all want our birthday meal to be: perfect food with someone we love, without anyone making a fuss. That's why I will remember it long after I cannot remember what age I am."

An affair
of the heart,
lung and liver

When your upcoming birthday ends in a five or a seven, people say things like, 'Which do you need more of—socks or underwear?' But when it ends in a nought, they go mad. So there's my nearest and dearest suddenly saying, 'If you could celebrate your birthday in any restaurant, anywhere in the world, where would you go?'

She meant it, too. A three-star in Paris, somewhere on the Amalfi coast, a kaiseki restaurant in Tokyo, bills in Darlinghurst, whatever. The last time I had a nought birthday, a limo turned up at the door to take me to what I thought was yum cha. I ended up whale-watching in Maui and drinking champagne at Jeremiah Tower's Stars restaurant in San Francisco, so I took her offer seriously.

But restaurants that are special enough to stand up to a nought birthday are few and far between. First to mind is the legendary Chez Panisse in San Francisco, the controversial Gordon Ramsay in London, and Gualtiero Marchesi's incurably romantic L'Albereta in Northern Italy. I could go to Restaurant Alain Ducasse in Paris, of course, but the poor man has enough on his shoulders simply retaining his reputation as the world's finest chef without having to cope with the added pressure of a nought birthday from Australia.

Then it hit me. It has been fifteen years since I stumbled upon one of the most remarkable restaurants in the world. A century-old Roman trattoria, Checchino dal 1887, sits on Monte Testaccio in an unfashionable quarter of Rome, opposite what was once the old slaughterhouse.

Positioned on a hill built up of broken wine and oil clay amphorae piled up by Roman slaves (perfect wine cellar insulation, as it turns out), Checchino has been in the same family for five generations. What makes the place remarkable is that most of the menu is given over to offal. The place is practically a shrine to the adoration of mysterious meats; a temple to funny bits; a memorial to discards.

In the early days, the abattoir slaughterers (*i vaccinari*) were given the meat off-cuts, known as the *quinto quarto* or 'fifth quarter' of the beast, as a supplement to their wages. They began to bring their wobbly, bumpy, strange-looking inner bits across the road to the fledgling *osteria* where the owners Lorenzo and Clorinda and their gifted daughter Ferminia transformed them into minor miracles. Ferminia's ingenious offal dishes made the tavern famous throughout Rome, and she is even credited with inventing the famous *coda alla vaccinara* or braised oxtail.

These very same dishes live on today in Checchino, under the supervision of her great, great grandsons, Elio and Francesco Mariani, and their mother Ninetta.

As the taxi pulls up outside Checchino in time for Sunday lunch, the late winter sunshine plays upon the rust-coloured stucco of the old trattoria, lighting it up like, well, a birthday cake. My mind is swimming with delicious visions of past delights: the delicate rigatoni with *pajata* (calves' intestines), the melt-in-the-mouth tripe, and the sweetbreads, kidneys and brains.

Inside, the room is deceptively simple, like a well-tailored suit that has lasted the distance. There is a sense of modest elegance hovering over the cashmere-clad crowd, as Elio pours wine, Francesco hovers, and Signora Mariani sits, smiling sweetly, by the cash register. Her favourite flower, the yellow rose, sits on every table in a gleaming Nonino grappa bottle.

While I don't quite believe the charming Francesco when he insists he remembers me from fifteen years ago, I am prepared to simply wallow in his easy hospitality. A request for a local red wine, something difficult to find in Rome, is a pleasure here, where nearly all the wines are red. Francesco disappears into the amphorae-lined cellar and returns with a Falesco 96 Monticino Rosso Lazio, an organic wine from nearby Montefiascone (home of Est Est Est) made by genius winemaker Ricardo Coterella.

The attention paid to the wine is remarkable. Francesco opens the bottle, checks the cork, then pours a little of the wine into a tasting glass, which he tastes and checks. Satisfied, he then pours a little more wine into one of our glasses, then swirls it around and pours it into the second glass. This in turn is swirled vigorously, before the wine is poured into the glasses at the table.

The process is called '*a vinare*', to 'wine' the glass. 'We do this because the glass may still hold the taste of the water or the soap, or even the scent of the shelf,' he says. 'By rinsing it with wine, it tastes of nothing but wine.'

Checchino is even fussier with the food. An *insalata di zampi* is a simple, delicately dressed salad of veal trotter meat, carrots, beans and crunchy celery. A small serve of *bucatini alla gricia* is a rustic-but-refined hollow pasta tossed with rendered pigs' cheek (*guanciale*) and crumbled ewes' milk cheese. Perfect. On the side, *puntarelle con salsa d'alici* is every Roman winter meal's accompaniment of chicory in anchovy sauce.

More red wine. More food. *Pajata in umido* is a lush, unctuous, stewy dish of calves' intestines that has the complexity of the ages in every bite.

The dish of the day, however, is a *griglia mista* like no other mixed grill in the world. It features a little curl of delicate spinal marrow, tasting for all the world like clotted cream, a small tangle of calves' intestines, velvety veal brains, almost spreadable sweetbreads, and a slash of melt-in-the-mouth liver. There is a sweetness and a liveliness that makes every mouthful a revelation, making up for all those tastebuds that die with every passing year.

I finish on a remarkable old-but-new combination of

gorgonzola drizzled with wild honey, served with a glass of Marsala, and alas, the meal is over. It is time for a walk though the old Jewish quarter, a coffee somewhere, and a snooze.

By now, the families with their well-dressed children have gone, and only a few tables linger over dessert wine and cheese. Checchino has come to the world's attention in the past few years, but there are remarkably few tourists at Sunday lunch, which is more of a Roman thing. Apparently the rave reviews in New York and London often gloss over the fact that Checchino is an offal specialist. Francesco sighs when people try to order fish and ravioli, but will not kowtow to the pressure.

'We won't do fish and ravioli for the tourists,' he says. 'You must have enough culture to know what you are doing and why you are doing it. We do this for our family, and we have been doing it for one hundred years.'

That's why Checchino is special, and that's why my birthday meal will be remembered long after I cannot remember what age I am. It was what we all want our birthday meal to be: perfect food with someone we love, without anyone making a fuss.

Besides, I was in a restaurant that is more than a century old, in a city that lives in, on and around the most ancient of monuments, in a country that thinks of the Renaissance as yesterday. It was easy to forget about silly little birthdays with noughts.

"I don't want sex on a plate. Don't we have enough trouble with sex in the bed, on the floor and up against the wall, without having it off on our plates as well?"

Tonight's dinner is rated R

t is no longer enough for food to be delicious, appetising, complex, hearty, mouth-watering, salty, aromatic, lip-smacking, long-flavoured, dainty, juicy, succulent, palatable, tangy, tasty, tender, savoury, sweet, spicy, saporific, pungent, fragrant, mouth-filling, fall-off-the-bone or just plain filling.

Instead, it has to be sensuous, seductive, voluptuous, full-bodied, loose-living, lustworthy, lush, luscious, wicked, desirable, solicitous, stimulating, sultry, satiny, silky, dreamy, gorgeous, flirtatious, naughty, racy, tantalising, teasing, provocative, and sex on a plate.

Well, call me a party-pooper, but I don't want sex on a plate. Don't we have enough trouble with sex in the bed, on the floor and up against the wall, without having it off on our plates as well?

I'm not talking about powdered deer horn, Spanish fly, ginseng, deer's penis or the testicles of a bull fresh from a bullfight. Aphrodisiacs are good for a giggle every now and then, and for a few limp gags around St Valentine's Day, but that's about it. I'm not even talking about chocolate. I'm talking about the family dinner, pea and ham soup, lamb chops, mashed potatoes and peas. The average five-year-old does not yet look up from his or her beef stew with potatoes, and say, 'Thanks Mum, that looks pretty sexy', but it can only be a matter of time.

A top-flight chef recently described a new dish on his menu as better than sex. This says more to me about the chef than his cooking. My mind still curdles at the memory of a junior food reviewer, unable to describe the excellence of the house-made pumpkin ravioli in any other terms than that it caused him to have an orgasm at the table. Not only do I feel enormous sympathy for his fellow diners on the evening in question, I have not been able to eat at that particular restaurant since.

Then, when they put London's Marco Pierre White on the cover of the now-defunct *Taste* magazine with a headline that read 'And he cooks, too', it was the beginning of the end.

It is now an unspoken rule that chefs have to be sexy too. Talent scouts hang around the dishwasher waiting to spot the next star of stove and screen. Hotel kitchens don't poach staff from each other any more, they simply ring a casting agency and get the chef's books sent over. Here he is holding a fish. Here he is leaning suggestively over the bananas. Here he is, his long fingers dripping with melted chocolate. And yes, it's always he. Female chefs don't seem to feel the need to be as appetising as their food.

America has now gone too far, with a series of ads showing famous chefs naked with their blenders. The first features the 54-year-old Jean-Louis Palladin completely in the buff, save for his strategically held Vita-Mix.

'You are a chef, you are a sex symbol, it is a part of life,' he told the *New York Times*.

So goodbye balding, paunchy, jolly chefs, and hello skinny, sexy, charming, glamorous media stars who can cook, too. After hundreds of years of being the anonymous, sweating, underpaid slave out the back, the chef's revenge is to be steamier than his puddings, and more desirable than his petits fours.

After all, you can gain access to a chef far more easily than a rock star or Hollywood star. Your desire can be sated. You can simply book a table, and go and eat his food, if not his body.

You can lurk by the kitchen delivery door, hoping for a glimpse, maybe snaring a used dish cloth as a souvenir. My wife has an old pinafore of Marco's that he threw at her across the heads of his diners in Harvey's many years ago as a token of his esteem. She laughs about it, but I notice she has kept it, and—even more telling—she has never washed it.

Now that chefs are being packaged by publishers and producers, they are used in fashion spreads and charity brochures. They have agents, for heaven's sake. You can book them for personal appearances, TV shows, and talkback shows. Then, of course, there is the culinary equivalent of a literary autobiography, the cookbook. Look at the titles alone: *White Heat*, *Your Place or Mine?*, *The Naked Chef*, *Intercourses*. Are you starting to feel manipulated yet? A little aroused, maybe?

Of course, we believe Jamie Oliver when he says the naked bit refers to stripping food back to the essentials. Sure it does, Jamie. Now button up your shirt, there's a good boy.

Upping
the anti

When the Italians get something wrong, they do it quite spectacularly. Look at—well, their government. But more importantly, take their antipasto. It's an inspired way of eating that transforms raw and cooked vegetables, seafood and simple cured meats into something irresistible.

I'm not talking about leathery salami, stuffed egg and giardiniera from a jar antipasto. Nor am I referring to those breathtaking Renaissance-style antipasto displays at our more florid Italian restaurants.

I'm talking more about a simple way of eating that involves sitting around a table, sipping a little wine, nibbling a little chargrilled this, a bit of marinated that and some freshly picked whatever, dressed simply in olive oil and lemon juice.

But the Italians insist that antipasto comes 'anti'—before—the 'pasto'—the meal. Wrong, wrong, wrong.

"Tradition dictates that antipasto is followed by a brodo, a pasta or a risotto, a solid main course, a salad, some cheese and dessert. Tradition is, of course, the size of a house."

Any sensible person who has ever indulged in antipasto knows that it *is* the meal. They should call it *invece di pasto*, 'instead of the meal'.

Tradition dictates that antipasto is followed by a brodo, a pasta or a risotto, a solid main course, a salad, some cheese, and dessert. Tradition is, of course, the size of a house. That's not a meal. That's a wedding banquet. By the time you get to the tiramisu end of things, you are so bloated and food-lagged you go a bit dippy, and think that a bowl of sweetened coffee-flavoured mascarpone cream with soggy biscuits is a good thing to eat.

Antipasto — with its Mediterranean counterparts of tapas, mezethes, mezes, whateverezes — is close to the perfect meal, with its own checks and balances, its own glorious contrasts of flavour, texture, colour and aroma, and its own ease of preparing and serving. It is complete in itself. What's more, you get to eat from as many as a dozen plates instead of just one. You've got me.

In the Italian homes I've been in, eating has a rhythm of its own. There might be a few olives on the table as people gather. Then a glass of wine is poured, which necessitates something more substantial, so some thinly sliced prosciutto is unwrapped. That calls for some crusty bread, and some extra-virgin olive oil, and maybe a fresh melon or pear. More people arrive, so out come platters of grilled vegetables, roasted red and yellow peppers, some fresh bocconcini cheese. Somebody's favourite jar of something will inevitably be opened and left hospitably on the table. Another glass of wine goes by, and it's time for something warm—a platter of gratinated mussels, some deep-fried zucchini flowers, a few grilled sardines, or maybe a warm frittata. Then, really, it's all over bar sitting around picking at a wedge of aged Parmigiano-Reggiano or some grapes, with plenty of time for an espresso coffee and a crisp cantuccini biscuit, as the matriarch apologises for the meagreness of the meal.

I would like to suggest that antipasto is a better way of eating than the one we have now. I don't mean the ingredients must be relentlessly Mediterranean, just that we could perhaps move towards the collective shared meal and away from the tyranny of the individual portion.

So tonight, I'm going to sit down to a table on which is laid a platter of fresh asparagus, a few pork sausages, split on the diagonal and chargrilled until sizzling, and a bowl of potatoes roasted with rosemary and garlic. There might be a perfect tomato or two, sliced and doused with good olive oil and red wine vinegar, and perhaps some zucchini, sliced lengthwise and lightly grilled. Okay, so it's only a whisker away from last week's sausages and mash, but the differences are greater than the staple products.

Instead of the culinary poverty of a heap of meat and a heap of starch with no room for anything else on the crowded plate, I am faced with a dazzling, brightly coloured display of all that is fresh and in season. Instead of the focus being on the selfish, individual serve, it is on the bigger picture, the assembled array.

Suddenly, it is a meal to share, to enjoy, to relax with, to talk over. It is a way of eating that removes us from the animal level, hunched and growling over one's own bone, and takes us to the higher realm of a sociable animal, able to put our bones on the table in the spirit of generosity, trust, hospitality and goodwill. So stop hogging the prosciutto, and start passing the olives.

"I have never cooked a single thing from the *Official Star Trek Cooking Manual*, for instance, not even the Vulcan vegetable curry. Just didn't get around to it."

Booked out

'm going to have to do something about my cookbooks. The walls seem to be closing in on me. Cookbooks now occupy three sides of my home office, most of the attic, and sundry cupboards. What's more, they keep popping up in the strangest places—under the bed, next to the bath, in the boot of the car, even in the kitchen.

Not only that, but they're breeding. I swear that when I wake up in the morning, there are more cookbooks than there were when I went to sleep. I'm convinced Nigella is having it off with Marco, that Antonio is chatting up Stephanie, and Robert Carrier, shocking flirt that he is, is getting up to no end of mischief. And I don't even want to think about the things Delia, Donna, Neil, Rick and Jamie get up to when I leave the room, but you can bet your life it's sticky.

The trouble is, my cookbooks are my family, my children, my love. I am genetically incapable of tossing one in the bin. If I buy one, I buy four; it's sort of compulsive. People know I collect them, so they give me heaps of them for Christmas and birthdays. A few friends have been down-sizing lately, and leave boxes of cookbooks on my doorstep. Lately, publishers have been sending me books to review, although they're not necessarily the ones I would buy. And every time I leave the country, I buy cookbooks as if they were postcards. So I've gone from nought to 3000 in twenty years. That means—let me see, using all fingers—I have averaged a gain of 150 cookbooks a year, or roughly a new one every second day.

But the time has come to admit that I no longer control my cookbooks. They control me. If I cooked something new for breakfast, lunch and dinner every day for the rest of my life, I still wouldn't be able to use them all. I have never cooked a single thing from *The Official Star Trek Cooking Manual*, for instance, not even the Vulcan vegetarian curry. Just didn't get around to it.

Nor have I ever cooked from *The New Hotdog Cookbook*, in spite of its irresistible promise: 250 new and exciting ways to fix this old-time favourite. Nor have I done anything but browse through *A Gourmet's Book of Beasts*, although the minute I find fresh armadillo in the local butcher, I'll have the onions, garlic, green peppers, ham, marjoram and pepper ready to go.

As for the gorgeous glossies in the shops, aren't you finding that a lot of modern cookbooks are starting to look the same? They seem to share the same fabulously talented handful of photographers, editors and stylists, and, let's be honest, recipes. Hummus, salmon fishcake, polenta, Thai salad, cod with a herb crust, duck with noodles, poached pears, flourless chocolate cake. Oh goody, another recipe for summer pudding.

Luckily, the publishers are making it easier for me, by bringing out lots of books I don't want. What on earth drives people to write some of these books? I once eagerly turned to the author's introduction in a book on salad dressings to discover what deep, dark compulsion forced her to explore the nether reaches of vinaigrette.

'When I was asked to write about salad dressings,' she wrote, 'I thought, why not?' Why not. There, in two words, were the grand, luxurious heights of her commitment, passion and philosophy.

So from now on, a cookbook has to *earn* its place on my shelves. It has to have something to say; it has to say it well; it has to have recipes that actually work; and it has to have a reason to be, other than 'why not'. The good ones have a sense of their time and place, and always leave you with a great idea or two. The bad ones are anonymous, international orphans designed for an anonymous, international market.

My new strategy is called Buy One, Set One Free. For every cookbook I bring into the house, I have to lose one from my collection. It's going to make me think pretty hard about buying something called *The Feng Shui Cookbook* (Creating health and harmony in your kitchen), or *Napkins, The Unfold Story*, believe me, if it means I will have to get rid of *The Official Star Trek Cooking Manual*.

"The true measure of good cooks isn't in cupboards bulging with gourmet packets, shelves lined with cookbooks or counters displaying gleaming couscousières. It's what they don't have."

Cupboard love

We start with nothing, and we end with nothing. But in the meantime, we have to surround ourselves with an awful lot of funny little jars, cans and bottles to keep going.

Even in the twenty-first century, we still need something as quaint and as old-fashioned as a pantry in order to survive. Pantry, larder, food cupboard—it all sounds hopelessly anachronistic, yet the idea of keeping a supply of useful, versatile basics has never made more sense. After all, what is a pantry but a whole range of pickled, canned, dried, bottled and salt-cured security blankets?

One of the most logical reasons for having a well-stocked pantry is that you don't have to put on your shoes and go down to the corner store and pay a fortune for something with an expired use-by date when you suddenly find you need it.

So you stock up on bamboo shoots, water chestnuts, soy sauce, dried chillies, dried mushrooms, noodles, jasmine rice, oyster sauce, crisp-fried shallots, rice wine, Sichuan peppercorns, Thai fish sauce and sesame oil. You make sure you have plenty of pasta, tomato purée, anchovy fillets, capers, olives, olive oil, arborio rice, canned beans, Indian spices, couscous and harissa.

And so on, until you have a kitchen cupboard bulging with packets and tins and jars and bottles. Security at last. But no, there are so many damned packets and tins and jars and bottles that you can't find anything you're looking for, so you have to put on your shoes and go down to the corner store and pay a fortune for something with an expired use-by date.

The true measure of good cooks isn't in cupboards bulging with gourmet packets, shelves lined with pricey cookbooks, or counters displaying gleaming couscousières and espresso machines. It's what they don't have.

They have acquired something more precious than saffron threads or truffle oil: the knowledge of what they don't need. They know the things that are important to them, and they stick to them. They can walk down a supermarket aisle and head straight to the things they want, forsaking all others. It's very admirable. But what about the rest of us?

If you're having trouble shutting the kitchen doors, or you've just left the oldies to start out on your own, or you're suddenly single and starving, it's time you, too, took stock of the vexing question of stocking up.

First, ignore all the books and magazines that give you a list of things you need. They don't eat the same stuff you do. For what do you need pine nuts and self-raising flour? You buy pesto and you don't bake.

Let's assume, then, that like most of us, you live on a happy mix of Mediterranean and Asian with a few old favourites thrown in. Next, pretend you are going to a holiday house. Whatever you would pack to take with you is really all you will ever need. Tea, coffee, eggs, milk, bread, butter. Sugar, salt, pepper, vodka. The rest is up to you and your particular desires, but if you don't need it during three weeks on holidays, you're not going to need it for twelve months at home.

Here, for the record, are the bare essentials as I see them. You only need two oils (extra-virgin olive and peanut) and two vinegars (red wine and Japanese rice). Sauces are another matter. Paring it right down, you can get away with soy sauce, Thai fish sauce, chilli sauce, tomato ketchup and a good mango chutney. Add mustard and whole egg mayonnaise if you're a sandwich-maker.

Anchovy fillets are critical, as are salted capers and dried Asian mushrooms.

You can't have too many cans of tomatoes or canned tuna or beans (borlotti, cannellini, whateveri). Then there are noodles, pasta, rice (arborio and jasmine), couscous and stock — either frozen or long-life — plus instant dashi.

Add the essential packet(s) of chocolate biscuits and you're ready to handle any emergency from a late-night snack attack to dinner for six. From that one intelligently stocked pantry you can put together literally hundreds of different meals. Throw at it a bit of fresh chicken, lamb chop, fish fillet or some Chinese cabbage and there are hundreds more.

There is also room to add exciting new pantry friends (that gorgeous lime pickle, that seductively crunchy peanut butter), and yet not lose track of old ones. There is inspiration as well as simple sustenance, pleasure as well as mere provision. Now, if only we could do the same with our wardrobes, life would be perfect.

■
Skin deep

People who surgically remove the crisp skin from their seared salmon are as bad as people who don't drink. They're not people you want to have in your life. Heaven knows how they approach other basic and fundamental skin-related activities such as you-know-what. No doubt they use euphemisms like you-know-what all the time.

Clearly, those who like skin — the infamous Hannibal Lecter apart — are decent, intelligent people in touch with their feelings. Happily, this accounts for ninety per cent of the human race.

Why else would roast suckling pig be the guest of honour at every Chinese banquet? It's not because everyone wants to eat a lot of pork. It's the skin thing; that divinely toasty, crisp crunch, like crispbread that's bad for you.

It's why the Sunday roast pork is such a favourite. The meat is just something you have to sludge through in

"The French, long acknowledged as the skincare specialists of the world, have ways of making chicken skin as glamorous as Beatrice Dalle, with dark coins of black truffle showing through like fresh bruises."

order to reward yourself with a mouthful of crisp, bub-bled crackling. The skin is the diva of the performance, sizzling in the spotlight, as the apple sauce plays sweet soprano and gravy the murky baritone.

The Chinese can also take credit for skin's finest hour, Peking duck. Here we have the very pinnacle of human ingenuity. How long did it take to work out that one had to baste the skin in a mixture of maltose and soy, then pierce a hole in the skin under the wing so the whole thing could be blown up like a balloon to separate the skin from the flesh? The result, after roasting, is edible lacquer – a brittle, aristocratically shiny skin that begs to be snuggled up with spring onion and cucumber in a baby blanket of pancake. The rest of the duck is okay, but it's hardly the point of the exercise.

The French, long acknowledged as the skincare specialists of the world, have ways of making chicken skin as glamorous as Beatrice Dalle, underlaid with a moisturising layer of forest-green tarragon farce, or with dark coins of black truffle showing through like fresh bruises. The skins from duck and goose necks become things of beauty when stuffed and formed into plump sausages by the master charcutiers of Paris and Lyons. In Gascony and the south-west, crunchy scrolls of crisply rendered duck skin (*graisserons*) are tossed through green salads, providing a luscious, lavish edge and richly tex-tural counterpoint. In Bologna, the skin of the pig's trotter takes on greatness as the casing for zampone, one of the few boiling sausages in the world that comes with toes.

In Japan, there is a subtle, disciplined way of salt-grilling sea bream so that the skin becomes something other than skin.

Mandarin or tangerine skin is revered by the Chinese, when dried to a crisp and then reconstituted to release its flavour in long, slow braises of pork, beef and duck. Grated lemon skin (zest) is a wake-up call for the tastebuds in a gremolata for osso buco, in vinaigrettes and in delicate madeleines.

Translucent beancurd skin, skimmed off the surface of something as innocent as coagulated soybean milk, nevertheless feels horrifically human to the touch. Its untanned dimpled texture and lifelike suppleness make it the perfect wrap for Malaysian popiah rolls, if you can get over the feeling that you're holding something warm and living in your hand.

Most people are in denial about skin. They peel it off and chuck it in the bin as if it were mere packaging. But clean, unpeeled fruit and vegetables not only retain more dignity, they also retain more nutritional goodness. Pumpkin and potatoes roasted in their skins have more flavour, tomatoes are fruitier and apples are crunchier. As for peeling grapes in order to serve them with game, there should be a law against it.

Skin is more than just 'the thing that keeps your insides in', as American comic Allan Sherman sang. It's the skin that's the beautiful thing. Beauty is, after all, only skin deep.

appetite & flavour

"Generally speaking, if I'm in a group of well-dressed people having a drink and I eat something marvellous, like a fresh chicken sandwich, I know someone has died."

Party politics

Nobody should be forced to eat food they can't see. There I was on the barely moonlit balcony of my host's palatial home at a prestigious A-list (well, A-minus) cocktail party, when I was offered a plate of dark triangular things. Two glasses of sparkling wine down and no dinner in sight, I was desperate enough to eat one.

'What was that?' hissed a voice from the shadows to my left.

'Um,' I said, trying to be helpful.

'Pizza? Quiche? Carpaccio?' The voice got hostile. 'What did it taste like?'

'Er,' I said. 'Triangular.'

Moving into the light, I found it did nothing but illuminate the fact that all the food at this particular cocktail party was either deep-fried, soggy, toxic or all three. Some of it, like the inevitable drawstring purses of wontons, had been deep-fried earlier in the day and reheated in the oven, which made their little purse tops as crunchy as discarded razor blades. Some of it had been deep-fried earlier in the day and not reheated, which made it soggy. Then there was the 'spicy blackened tuna', which was like putting a mini crematorium in one's mouth. And taking it out again immediately after. Thank heavens we were on a balcony.

The night before that was a magazine launch, on a floating pavilion whipped by bitter winds. The waiters carried long gondola-shaped trays lined with small deep-fried things, and cried out 'incoming' as they launched their spear-headed weapons into the heart of each swarm of guests. Others carried long bamboo tubes in which were inserted bamboo cones of deep-fried cuttlefish and chopsticks. You took a cone in one hand, and the chopsticks in the other, and held your glass in the other. Yeah, right. Then there was nowhere to put the empty cone when you had finished. Thank heavens we were on a floating pavilion.

I am seriously considering never attending another book launch, gallery opening, child's christening, birthday drinks, office get-together, unveiling, dedication, fashion preview or any social gathering of any kind that vaguely resembles a cocktail party. Excepting a wake, because people always get fed properly at a good wake. Generally speaking, if I'm in a group of well-dressed people having a drink and I eat something marvellous, like a fresh chicken sandwich, I know someone has died.

It's time we had a quiet word in the ear of the caterers. Ratatouille is *not* a finger food. Neither is risotto. Nor is Thai green chicken curry. Tart shells tend to go soft when filled early in the morning and left to stand until the cocktail hour. Nori rolls need something in them as well as rice to make them interesting. Spicy blackened tuna is not a good idea.

To anyone planning a big-budget event in the immediate future, I have three words for you: oysters and Champagne. And three more: lots of both.

The genesis of the cocktail party can be traced back to all those birthday parties we attended as children. You remember — you dress up in something silly and uncomfortable that you're not allowed to get dirty, and you are forced to talk to people you have nothing in common with except your age. You get over-excited, drink too much and probably throw up on the way home. The pattern was set.

Yet by the time the next party rolled around, some deeply diabolical, biological function programmed us to forget the burst balloons, the dropped cake and the broken presents. Suddenly there we were again, standing still while Mum combed a neat part in our hair, getting excited all over again. That pattern, too, was set.

Because, now that I come to think of it, those eggshell-thin, crisp pastry tarts with the cauliflower cream topped with caviar at the charity auction last week were quite dreamy. As for tonight's retrospective, and tomorrow night's new mobile phone launch, I find myself quite looking forward to them.

"We get to choose whether we leave the onion out, or put the beetroot in, or double the mayonnaise. The humble sandwich gives back a little of the control over our lives that convenience foods take away."

Spread
the word

Meat pies roll off assembly lines. The pizza has degenerated into an automated piece of me-too engineering with indecipherable toppings, and hamburgers are cloned into identical polystyrene coffins.

A sandwich, on the other hand, is one of the few things left in life that allows us to exert our individualism. A sandwich is action food, with much of the action left firmly in our own capable hands.

That's why the words 'made to order' are so compelling. We get to choose whether we leave the onion out of our salad sandwich, or put the beetroot in, or double the mayonnaise. In this way, the humble sandwich gives back a little of the control over our lives that convenience foods take away.

The best sandwiches in all the world can be found in a very sophisticated sandwich bar in Vienna by the name of Trzesniewski (at Dorotheergasse 1), pronounced correctly by sneezing as you say Trezneeyevskee. Here, the counters groan under the weight of giant trays full of rich, delicate open-faced sandwiches spread with a mixture of egg and mayonnaise, and flavoured with ham, lobster, mushroom, herring, goose liver, salmon or capsicum. There are no tables and chairs, just a couple of counters to lean on, but the sandwiches are irresistible. Stay for a fresh goose liver roll and whistle up a *pfiff* (125 ml or $4\frac{1}{2}$ fluid ounces) of beer.

Then there is the mighty club sandwich, or rather the good hotel guide sandwich, for by far the best way to judge the quality of a hotel is to order a club sandwich as soon as you check in.

The best club sandwich in the world, however, is not in a hotel but at Venice's renowned Harry's Bar. There, they are grilled, butter side up, and filled with bacon, home-made mayonnaise, cos lettuce, tomato, shredded poached chicken, salt, pepper and, for the final touch, a few drops of Worcestershire sauce. That's not sandwich-making, that's art.

If the sandwich has a spiritual home, it has to be America, for it was here, between the wars, that sandwich-making developed into an unashamed national obsession. Ever since, Americans have been able to take anything and slap two slices of bread around it.

The advent of the automobile (there were twenty-six million in America by 1930), meant there were millions of mouths on the road, ready to pull over and feed in roadside eateries and at scenic viewing stops. Aided by the invention of the one-pound butter pack (1922), the toaster (1924) and sliced bread (1928), the sandwich spread like peanut butter throughout the land. Regional variations grew, and took on exotic war-like names like hero, hoagy, wedgie, torpedo, bomber, rocket, zeppelin and sub.

The height of American sandwich-serving can be found today in the high-rise pastrami sandwich eaten with much relish (both spiritual and material) at the 110-year-old Katz's Deli in New York (205 East Houston Street). It's a great place, full of old codgers who are as rude as one would wish.

'Where you from, buddy?' asked my last waiter. I told him.

'How much did it cost you to get here?' he asked. I told him.

'Here,' he said, pulling a few dollars out of his pocket. 'Go home.'

Katz's Deli is also famous for being the spot where Harry met Sally. Mind you, if Harry had met Sally in London, it would have been over a salt beef-on-rye at London's Harvey Nichols' Fifth Floor sandwich bar, where the charming Dylis wields a sharp knife instead of a rapier wit.

So what's your favourite sandwich? Come on, everyone has one. For the Earl of Sandwich, it was cold meat. For the late American cookery author, James Beard, it was the club. For Elvis Presley, it was a pan-fried peanut butter and banana sandwich made by his personal cook, Mary Jenkins.

For the writer Kurt Vonnegut, it's peanut butter and pickle on rye. For Dolly Parton, it is a smoky barbecue sandwich. For me, it's mortadella (*dolce*, not *piccante*) on sourdough (crust on), spread with butter (salted, not unsalted) and topped with cheese (provolone), artichoke hearts (preserved in olive oil), tomatoes (oven-roasted, not sun-dried) and mayo (whole egg, unsweetened). With sandwiches, simple is always the way to go.

■
The unsung herb

Garnish with parsley, add basil, tuck in the mint leaves, scatter with finely chopped chives, toss with garlic and rosemary. Where the hell, in this litany of cooking clichés, is the marjoram?

Nowhere to be seen, and that's the story of its life. Ever since it missed out on being in the song—parsley, sage, rosemary and Not Marjoram—it has been left on the shelf, in the pot and down the garden path. It's a regular wallflower—well actually it's a perennial *Labiatae*—but you get my drift.

Marjoram must be used to being the invisible herb by now, cold-shouldered by a century of cooks. Is it in that timeless French flavouring for braised meats and stews, the bouquet garni? No. The classic bouquet garni is parsley, thyme and a bay leaf, and that's it. Nor is it sufficiently refined to join the famous *fines herbes* of the French kitchen. Chic chervil is there of course, the

"Ever since it missed out on being in the song–parsley, sage, rosemary and Not Marjoram–it has been left on the shelf, in the pot and down the garden path. It's a regular wallflower."

cheffiest herb of them all, and sparky little chives, and aniseedy tarragon and the ubiquitous parsley, but not sweet little marjoram.

The only place you might find it, shrivelled and dry and lacking in joy, is in a jar of commercial 'mixed herbs', rubbing shoulders with all sorts of dead weeds.

Marjoram's failure to bring itself to our attention is merely a result of its own character: polite, delicate, sweet. It smooths out the edges of those rough-and-tough Mediterranean herbs, linking the flavours in a gently manipulative manner, rather as a diplomatic corps hostess moves around the room massaging egos and framing mutually beneficial introductions.

Run through the index of Delia Smith's *How To Cook: Book One* and you'll find six entries for rosemary, three for basil, three for chives, two for parsley and one each for thyme and sage . But don't even bother looking under M. It's not there. Neither does it make an appearance in James Beard's American cookery nor in any of Donna Hay's three *Marie Claire* cookbooks.

The *Conran Cookbook* damns marjoram with faint praise, describing its smell as very sweet, yet when it comes to oregano, marjoram's vulgar cousin (*Origanum vulgare* as opposed to *Origanum marjorana*) out roll the superlatives. Oregano has 'a wonderfully warm, heady scent' and a 'strong spicy flavour'.

So heady oregano with its Mediterranean charm and its vulgar ways gets to pick up all the plum jobs, like flavouring pizza, pasta sauces and chilli con carne. What oregano misses out on (poultry stuffings) sage picks up. In the meantime, a prim and proper little miss marjoram is forced to eke out a living from odd jobs, like being scattered over a light cheese omelette just before folding, or being tossed through a salad of small green leaves.

She could go and look for work on the continent, up north in Scandinavia perhaps, or way over in Eastern Europe, but chives and dill have the game pretty well sewn up, and things could get a bit rough.

The reason I bring this up is because I have a garden full of the world's most unfashionable herb. Rampant would be the word. Shag-pile carpet springs to mind. Because marjoram has one overwhelming characteristic: any fool can grow it. Look at it and it will grow. Ignore it and it will flourish. It adores poor soil, and can take the sort of sunny position that would reduce more delicate herbs to compost.

Obviously, the reason I'm overrun with the stuff is that I'm not using it. Every pubescent basil leaf that shows its face is plucked immediately, the thyme gets ravaged whenever goats' cheese enters the house, and sage is sizzled in olive oil for its smell alone.

But I can't eat the number of omelettes that I would need to in order to make a dent in the marjoram. I could start dropping it into my soups at the last moment, and scattering it over buttered carrots, and slipping it into fish tummies, and stirring it through fresh ricotta cheese to have with crusty bread, but there is probably a limit to how much marjoram one can ingest. Or I could harvest great armfuls of the stuff and strew it over my floors as they did in pre-mat days, so that every step releases its sweet fragrance. But you know what would happen if I did that—it would just grow back, higher, greener and more fragrant than ever before.

It has to go. I'm going to rip the lot out and replant the beds with something new, inspiring and exciting. Like tansy, rue, savory and balm. There could even be a hit song in it.

"Now that I'm over my creamed corn era, my canned asparagus period and my pink marshmallow fixation, I run a very PC kitchen. Except for my *bête rouge*. It's tomato ketchup."

■ Hidden treasures

For some, it's the processed cheese slices. For others, it's the little plastic tubs of chocolate custard, the tube of condensed milk or last night's burger-and-chips.

We all have our guilty little secrets, and we all like to keep them as secrets. One knock on the door, and the first thought isn't 'Oh goody, who could be visiting little old me?' but 'Quick, hide the Coco Pops'.

Let's face it, there are some jars, packets and bottles that broadcast to the world that we're not as sophisticated, tasteful, eco-friendly or biodegradable as we'd like to believe we are. These double standards make every trip to the supermarket a potential journey into hell. You slip the family block of chocolate under the loo paper in the trolley, and the instant coffee behind the herbal tea. I'm even embarrassed about seeking out my low-kilojoule tonic water. Believe me, I wouldn't do it but for the fact that I drink so much vodka.

Paranoid about being outed for our bourgeois palates, we hide the debris of our everyday tastes at the backs of our cupboards and drawers. I have some friends who conduct an intensive bacon search before a certain aunt comes to visit. The whole refrigerator is frisked from top the bottom, eyes peeled for the merest hint of a bacon label or ham bone. It wouldn't be a big deal, except for the fact that she's Jewish, and so are they. Once, they even found her with her nose in the freezer.

People with children are luckier than most, because they can always blame the Tim Tams, Kraft cream cheese spread and industrial-sized jar of Nutella on the kids. I tried that too, until my friends reminded me there were no children in the house.

Now that I'm over my creamed corn era, my canned asparagus period and my pink marshmallow fixation, I run a very PC kitchen. Except for my *bête rouge*. It's tomato ketchup. I know it's a commercial, sweet, red, heavily advertised supermarket product, but there are things I like that I couldn't make without it.

I learned the secret of making Singaporean chilli crab, for instance, from the old woman who makes the best version in her little stall at Singapore's Newton Circus food centre. Was it because she used only the finest Sri Lankan mud crabs? No. Was it because she smoked her chillies before grinding them? No. Was it the fresh young hen's eggs she used to make the egg-flower sauce that draped over the dish like edible lace? No. It was the bottle of Heinz Tomato Ketchup she kept under the counter, and it made all the difference in the world.

I also have to find the bottle for Robert Carrier's kedgeree: a little leftover rice, hard-boiled egg, smoked fish, ham and a good dollop of ketchup, and you've suddenly made one of the Great Dishes of the World. And if I have some really good, fresh prawns, they still love to be dipped into a silky cocktail sauce, glowing rosily with ketchup.

But no matter where I put the bottle in the cupboard, it invariably makes its way to the rear. Either it's terminally shy or photosensitive, or my dear partner has opened the kitchen cupboard, gasped in outrage at the offending label, and flung it to the dim, dark recesses.

I have to hack my way, like a machete-wielding jungle fighter, through an undergrowth of Thai fish sauce, Italian balsamic vinegar, Australian mustard seed oil, Spanish olive oil, English mango chutney and German mustard just to get to my beloved ketchup.

What we eat in public isn't always what we eat behind closed doors. The café maven with his poetically disarranged hair and espresso attitude lives on mugs of tea-bagged tea at home. The restaurant critic pontificating on gently poached green lip abalone with Yunnan ham, truffle oil, hijiki seaweed and wasabi-flavoured flying fish roe does a fast line in crunchy peanut butter on toast when he/she gets home.

It makes my little bottle of tomato ketchup look positively innocent. Until I pour it all over my bacon-and-egg sandwich, that is.

"If you really want to have fun on a tabletop, cook on it. This is tabletop dancing the whole family can enjoy, as well as theatre sports for your friends."

Tabletop dancing

The best soup I have ever eaten took all night to make. Not only that, it took eight people to make it. It took at least twenty-five different ingredients, each added in no particular order, a little at a time. We didn't even leave the pot, but stayed there watching over it every second of the way.

In truth, we managed to pass the time chatting and laughing and drinking and eating and generally making a very nice evening of it.

In fact, we didn't even know at the time that we were making soup. We thought we were just eating dinner. It's just that dinner happened to be a Singaporean steamboat—a collection of thinly sliced raw meats, vegetables and fresh seafood all popped into little wire baskets and dunked into a brass pot of steaming stock which bubbled gently away on a gas burner in the middle of the table. When each bite-sized piece of food was cooked, it was then taken out, put in one's own bowl, and dipped into a gorgeous sauce lurking nearby.

It's a great way to eat. It's also a great way to cook.

By the end of the evening, the basic stock had been enriched by countless ceremonial dunkings of liver, pork, bok choy cabbage, fish balls, prawns, chilli, bitter melon, shiitake mushrooms, beancurd, spring onions and god knows what else. Our host then tipped a plate of softened rice vermicelli noodles into the pot and heated them through. The resulting noodle soup tasted fantastic, with a full, rounded quality that still managed to be fresh, light and balanced.

If you really want to have fun on a tabletop, cook on it. This is tabletop dancing the whole family can enjoy. It is also theatre sports for your friends, as they actively participate in the creation of their own meal. The excitement of sitting down at the prepared table, the fun of dipping and swooping and eating, the passing of plates and spoons, the furtive checking to see if you have missed out on anything, the fighting over whose little basket belongs to whom (when in doubt, yours is the closest), all add up to a strong bonding experience for a generation used to individual servings of burgers and fries.

It started for me in Singapore, at the dear departed original Singapore Satay Club, a mad, smoky open-air cluster of tables and stalls stretching out over reclaimed land near the Raffles Hotel, now a neo-forest of sky-scraper shopping centres and hotels.

So besotted was a friend with the Singaporean steamboat concept that he returned home and immediately

Ariel Booksellers
(02) 9332 4581
A.C.N. 003 954 014
A.B.N. 64003954014

Tax Invoice

SICK PUPPY		19.70
HUNGER		29.95
	Total less GST	45.14
	Total GST	4.51
	Total sale	49.65
Cash	Amount Tendered	50.00
	Change	0.35

9332 4581 04/11/00 14:58   92

Thank you

drilled a small hole in the middle of his walnut dining table to accommodate the tubing from a table-top gas burner leading to a large gas cylinder underneath. This was just before he found out about those cute little Japanese and Korean tabletop stoves that run on even cuter gas cartridges that slip into the side of the unit.

Scary? No, it's not scary at all. Even an unhandy man like me has yet to blow himself up with his dinner. It's not for lack of trying, either. Thanks to my trusty 'Sam Ho' cooker, I've been to Japan via *sukiyaki*, *shabu shabu* and *yosenabe*, the Japanese answer to *bouillabaisse*. I've been to Sichuan via a chilli-laden oil and stock hotpot. I've been to Korea via *bulgogi* (barbecued beef), and *haemul chongol* (seafood stew). I've even been to Switzerland via a fondue, but I may not get back there again for some time.

That slick little tabletop gas cooker is far more than just an emergency back-up unit for power brown-outs. It's a mini entertainment city in metal. Suddenly some of the world's truly great dishes are within your power. These are dishes your six-burner, industrial-strength, latest-model Scandinavian kitchen range is powerless to provide. Unless, of course, you can disconnect it and plonk it on top of your table.

By cooking your own food to the exact time you want it, exactly where you want it, you can feel completely in control of every aspect of your meal, and therefore (it's a short jump) your destiny. Best of all, you can send your compliments to the chef, and accept them gratefully at the same time.

"I love the vile-smelling liquid that gathers at the bottom of the barrel of rotten, stinking, fermented fish, leached out of the fish by salt as the bones gradually decay into dried skeletons."

Fishy
business

I do like a nice plate of smelly, dried-up, grey old fish every now and then. I love dried, salted cod, especially when reconstituted on the fashionable bistro menu into a soft, creamy paste prepared with milk, potatoes and herbs that the French know as *brandade*, and the Italians as *baccalà alla Mantecato*.

I love those little dishes of Bombay duck in Indian restaurants, the tiny dried fish bodies crunching in the mouth like dead men's bones. And I love the unneighbourly off smell and powerful flavour of belacan (blachan), a dark paste of sun-dried shrimps from Malaysia that comes in blocks that look like the devil's butter. I keep mine in an airtight glass jar, and check my watch every time I open it. Generally, it takes between five to seven minutes for Fatso, the fluffball of a cat next door, to peer cautiously over the fence.

Even better than smelly dried fish, however, is a

barrel of rotten, stinking, fermented fish. I love the vile-smelling liquid that gathers at the bottom of the barrel, leached out of the fish by salt as the fish bones gradually decay into dried skeletons. After three months of sitting out in the sun, the dark liquid is filtered, bottled and left to cure until it is the colour of dry sherry.

They call it fish sauce, or rather, *we* call it fish sauce — Thai people call it *nam pla* and the Vietnamese *nuoc mam* — and it is one of the most unusual and intriguing sauces to land on our tables in the past few years.

It tastes salty and fishy in a single splash, like a foetid rockpool on a hot afternoon, but it blends surprisingly easily into stir-fries and curries, adding bite to sauces, soups and salad dressings. It is the essential flavour of Thailand, allowing the lime juice to retain its tang, the chilli its bite, the lemongrass its fragrance, the tamarind its sourness and the coconut milk its creaminess.

This suddenly fashionable sauce has the same DNA as *garum*, the salty fermented anchovy sauce of ancient Rome. Two thousand years later, it could turn into the new salt. You can taste it lurking murkily in the background of the Asian-marinated roast turbot with cucumber and coriander salad in London's Sugar Club restaurant. It is also in New York, adding complexity to Jean-George Vongerichten's tuna spring roll with soy-bean coulis. And it's the secret of the vinaigrette that comes with your baby leaf salad on Qantas first and business class flights, thanks to chef Neil Perry of Sydney's much-lauded Rockpool restaurant. It is so moreish I had to ask for three extra helpings so I could pour it over everything.

And before you think this is all funny foreign stuff, take a look at a bottle of Worcestershire sauce the next time you slug some into a Bloody Mary. Stinking rotten fish, yet again. In this case, the smelly liquid obtained from salting small anchovies is mixed with chilli, ginger, shallots, garlic, vinegar, soy and molasses, and matured in oak barrels. It's the same thing, but it's English, so it's perfectly acceptable.

But you can't use Worcestershire sauce in your Thai salad or *pad Thai* noodles, and I'm not sure about sloshing fish sauce into your Bloody Mary, either. Fish sauce is unique. If you have a recipe that calls for it, you can always add salt, but you will only be adding salt, not a complex, matured essence ingeniously harvested from the sea.

I buy fish sauce the way I buy wine: by the label. The best belongs to the Golden Boy Brand, which features a plump, beaming baby surrounded by red and yellow sunbursts, sitting on a garishly coloured atlas while clutching a bottle of fish sauce in one hand and giving a resounding thumbs up with the other. You just have to trust a label like that.

My research has even turned up a claim that fish sauce is a natural protein additive used by nature in the formation of fish bone, and that it may prolong life, retarding the aging process. Don't you love it? The elixir of youth, the fountain of eternal freshness, lies in a bucket of rotten, stinking fish.

"Soufflés are made on the spot, for us alone, and last but a moment before us. The person who invents a soufflé that will keep warm for three hours deserves to be shot for disservice to dining."

Living for the *à la minute*

The daily special of nettle risotto caught my eye. 'I'm afraid,' said the waiter, 'that will take thirty minutes.'

'How wonderful,' I said, and promptly ordered it, safe in the knowledge that my risotto would be prepared from scratch, with all the necessary stirring, coddling and coaxing that separates a risotto from a limp pilaf.

Sure enough, when it came to the table, the grains of rice were cooked to just the right puff-chestedness, with the tiniest *al dente* heart. They were cloaked in a creamy film that just stopped short of being soupy, and that tasted like a living, breathing thing.

There is nothing more satisfying than food cooked *à la minute*, or to order. Correct Italian pasta can only be cooked '*espress*' or *espresso*, to be worthy of the name. Cooked in such a manner, it requires very little by way of extras, as it seems to have its own life essence intact.

The Chinese have their equivalent, in the 'breath of the wok', or *wok hei*. The essence of the Cantonese stir-fry hinges on throwing only the freshest ingredients into a searingly hot wok, and allowing them to be imbued with its 'breath'.

There is no *wok hei* to be found in your steamy, soggy, Oriental take-away food, or in warming trays of corn-floured sadness.

'Never kill a beast twice,' say the Chinese. They did not imagine a third, slow, lingering death in a stainless-steel tray universally known as a bain-marie.

While 'Mary's bath' was originally an alchemist's term, it soon became 'a utensil used for keeping sauces, soups or mixtures warm so that they can be used later' (*Larousse Gastronomique*), as well as a method of cooking delicate foods gently and slowly. Now it seems to be the catering equipment of the day, which is a distinct worry.

I see an over-populated future world in which the only way to feed the masses is from huge food-warming trays. But food from a bain-marie is extremely limited in gastronomic terms. It is neither hot nor cold, neither fresh nor stale.

Seemingly, the warming tray, chafing dish or bain-marie is something that only Indian food can survive. I'm not sure what that says about Indian food.

Obviously, if it were a truly good idea, we would have one at home. But we don't really want to cook something hot and delicious, and then put it in a tray and suspend it inside a larger tray of heated water and leave it for a few hours. We want to eat something hot, delicious and freshly prepared. That's why what we do is called home cooking, and not mass catering, because it's prepared by a loving cook for a grateful family just before said family descends upon it like greyhounds on the mechanical hare.

Many foods deteriorate visibly for every minute of their existence. The Japanese devised the sushi bar so the diners could sit as closely as possible to the source of the food, with many dishes being consumed within seconds of being made.

One of the reasons we all go ga-ga over soufflés is because they are made on the spot, for us alone, and last but a moment before us. The person who invents a soufflé that will keep warm for three hours is a person who deserves to be shot for disservice to dining. To put in one's order for a savoury or dessert soufflé, and then to wait a minute or two as the order goes into the kitchen, is truly a fine dining moment if rewarded with the tinny snare-drum rhythm of a whisk in a copper bowl.

In the future, science may well find a better way to cook than *à la minute*. But it's going to take a long time.

"You try restarting a warm, sexy pre-sorbet conversation when you are sitting there with a lump of ice in your mouth. All the mellowing of mood and setting up of appetite suddenly counts for nothing."

■
Ice rage

They were everywhere in the 1980s, when you least expected and wanted them. They would come totally without warning, with no menu listings and no staff cautions. Even now, you are never entirely safe.

There you are, having just polished off a perfectly nice crab ravioli with tomato, sage and lemon olive oil, enjoying the last of your 96 Domaine LaRoche Petit Chablis, looking forward to your salt-crusted squab with Indian spiced potatoes, shallot and sherry stock, when it lands in front of you.

'The sorbet tonight (or worse, 'the palate-refresher') is Champagne (or lemon verbena, or vodka, basil and tomato, or crushed angels' wings),' intones the waiter, then scampers before you can say 'melt in hell'.

Politely you sigh, and pick up your dinky, stupid little spoon. It is as if someone has just thrown an entire bucket of ice all over the table.

A sorbet doesn't refresh the palate, it freezes it, instantly destroying any lingering flavours and aromas that may still be wafting around from the entrée. It also kills the wine you were enjoying so much, suddenly leaving it with an alluring hint of aged aluminium on the back palate.

All that mellowing of mood and setting up of appetite suddenly counts for nothing, as the carefully structured timing and balance and magic of the meal is reduced to that of scoffing a sandwich in the car. You try restarting a warm, sexy pre-sorbet conversation when you are sitting there with a lump of ice in your mouth. You're history.

If you must refresh your palate (whatever that may mean) then I suggest you gargle with the last few drops of Petit Chablis. It is so much more romantic.

And don't try to tell me that chefs love to offer sorbets as cryogenic incarnations of their creativity. Let's not forget they happen to make money out of them. Not bad money either. Think about it—a little left-over Champagne and some sugar syrup churned together by the fourth-removed apprentice, and there you have it, money for jam.

They have also very neatly begged a bit more time in the kitchen, pacing the bulk of the high-pressure main courses until later in the evening. In other words, dragging out your meal.

That's the other thing I hate about sorbets. If I go out for a one-, two- or three-course meal, then that's what

I want. I don't want huge, hearty appetisers that ruin my entrée, and intra-course icy-poles that ruin my main course, and pre-dessert desserts that ruin my dessert. I want what I have come for, in the time I have allotted it.

Rather than a palate refresher, I suggest the sorbet be listed on the menu as a Profit refresher, or a Pace enhancer.

But it's all in the timing. Give me a delicate, fresh fruit sorbet at the end of the meal, and I'm a puppy. Scoop me a scoop of gelato or sorbetto flavoured with pomegranate, mint or pistachio, and stroll with me along the beachfront promenade of a southern Italian seaside village, and life is beautiful. Surprise me with icy glasses of coffee granita after fish and chips on the sand, and I'm yours forever.

Perhaps when the Florentines started putting freshly fallen snow into their wine glasses as a favourite dinner party trick a few hundred years ago, it was all terribly exciting. These days, however, the sorbet leaves me cold.

"Leftovers are a far better reason to go into the kitchen and cook than whatever it is you went in there to cook in the first place. They are proof that the modern mantra of freshness is not always desirable."

The second
time around

I f I had my way, all roast lamb recipes would end with
the words 'remove the lamb from the oven, allow to
cool, and refrigerate overnight'.

I suppose roast lamb is quite nice as it comes from the
oven, along with roast potatoes, pumpkin, parsnip, peas
and gravy, but it's much, much nicer, much, much later.

Besides, hot roast lamb is hot roast lamb, whereas
cold roast lamb can be an infinite number of things other
than cold roast lamb. It can be a sandwich of white crusty
bread, thin slices of lamb and spoonfuls of mustard
pickles. It can be a cottage pie, topped with leftover mash.
It can be lamb fritters to serve hot with home-made
tomato sauce.

Leftovers might be yesterday's heroes, but to many of
us they are a far better reason to go into the kitchen and
cook than whatever it is you went in there to cook in the
first place.

You can keep your Saturday night dinner party with Brooke and Rodney, and your reduced sauces and double-shelled broad beans and finest Riedel glasses. I'd rather be invited over on Sunday night to sit around the telly with the family, helping to polish off the leftovers.

The premiere of an opera or play is never as good as the third or fourth night when the nerves and self-consciousness have gone and the performers are oozing with well-crafted confidence.

Leftovers have seen the world, lived a little and swapped the impetuousness of youth for the wisdom of age. They are smarter, more rounded and far more giving than show-off, first-night food. 'And the lightly tossed salad of baby mizuna leaves is dressed tonight by Champagne vinegar and provençale hazelnut oil with a little touch of Dijon.'

Leftovers aren't pretty, but they make you feel good, which is surely the whole point of eating. They are proof that the modern mantra of freshness is not always desirable. Rows of flesh-pink little lamb chops, shiny, bouncy prawns, and glossy eat-me chocolate cakes in the shops will always be appealing, but I get more excited opening my fridge and finding a stack of plastic containers, and small enamel dishes covered in plastic wrap.

That platter of last night's risotto may not be very appealing now, but if I pan-fry it in a non-stick saucepan with a touch of olive oil and flatten it, I will have the most divine crisp cake of luscious melting rice to serve as a bed for something wonderful that I have yet to find in the back of the fridge. Or I might form it into balls with a little surprise of fresh bocconcini cheese inside, and deep-fry them until the cheese melts and goes all gooey.

Nobody would have invented pea and ham soup if they didn't have a leftover ham bone staring at them every time they opened the fridge door. We wouldn't have corn beef hash if we didn't have leftover corned beef. And don't even get me started on bread. Okay, so I'm already started: summer pudding; bread and butter pudding; croutons; bread crumbs; stuffings; indeed, life as we know it.

I know you're thinking that baking tray of clammy, claggy leftover mash doesn't look too promising. But then you're probably not Ukrainian, so you don't know you're looking at the start of *vareniki*, heavenly pockets of pasta stuffed with potato, sweetly cooked onion and a mountain of butter. You're not Italian, or you would know you're twenty minutes away from tucking into a bowl of soft, melting gnocchi with burnt butter sauce and shards of Parmigiano.

You're obviously not French, either, or you would be busy transforming it into light little potato crepes. And you certainly can't be English, or you would have turned it into fishcakes already.

It's time that leftovers came out of the cupboard—and the refrigerator, and the freezer and the bread bins—and into the spotlight where they belong. And for us all to realise one great, simple truth: there are never any leftovers when you cook leftovers.

"Once they have kneaded, pounded and pummelled their bread dough, it's time to relax. Keep going and they would get exhausted and eventually break down, which is exactly what would happen to their dough."

Rest assured

The first time a recipe told me to remove the chicken from the oven and let it rest for fifteen minutes, I took it outside and propped it up on the old banana lounge under the potted olive tree. Then I tucked a little towel over its knees, fixed it a gin and tonic, and read aloud from the latest John Grisham novel. It was very pleasant. I even dozed off at one point. But did it do anything at all for the chicken?

Yes. This resting business really works. If I had carved the poor bird immediately, the juices would have run out and I would have had tight, dry meat. It's these juices, more so than the cooking times, that give you succulent, tender meat. The heat of the oven forces the meat to tighten, squeezing the juices to the surface. After all, it had just been poked, prodded, trussed, stuffed and left to swelter in 200-degree heat for an hour or so. No wonder it felt a little tense and tight. Anyone would.

Give it time to relax, however, and a magical thing happens. The muscles relax and the juices flow back and re-irrigate the meat. The texture of the meat softens, giving that desirable melting tenderness. Resting also allows the collective heat from the outside of the meat to work its way into the middle, so the meat ends up more evenly cooked.

Exactly the same principle applies to fish, lamb, game and beef. Especially beef. Without the banana lounge treatment, you get roast beef with a red heart and a grey overcoat. With it, you get a uniform rosy pink from one end to the other and from one side to the other.

The most striking example of resting comes with what the Chinese call red-cooking or red-braising. Red-cooking is my new best friend. I now red-cook everything in sight, because, well, because it's so bloody simple. First, a piece of pork, beef or chicken is very gently simmered in a mixture of stock, soy sauce and Chinese rice wine, flavoured with star anise, cinnamon, ginger and garlic. That's the hard part.

The secret is in knowing the point at which you turn off the heat, allowing the second stage of cooking—that of cooling in the liquid—to take place. That's the easy part. After steeping in the cooling stock for an hour or two, the meat takes on an alluring caramel tan and a soft, juicy, silken texture.

The truly extraordinary thing about red-cooking is that it produces a master stock that has the ability to out-live you, as long as it keeps getting its rest. It just goes on getting richer and better with every use. So all you have to do is keep it in the fridge, remembering to bring it to the boil every three or four days to refresh it. Such master stocks have been known to be handed down from generation to generation.

Bakers, too, know the benefit of resting. Once they have kneaded, pounded and pummelled their bread dough, it's time to relax. Keep going and they would just get exhausted and eventually break down, which is exactly what would happen to their dough. When it's overworked, the dissulphide crosslinks are interrupted (that's bad) and the stuff becomes sticky and inelastic.

To fulfil its destiny, the dough needs to rest, covered, in a warm place, for an hour or so to ferment and rise. Left to its own devices, the dough begins to 'breathe', giving out carbon dioxide bubbles that cause the dough to double and even triple in size.

Both pasta dough and pastry need their beauty sleep before they can be transformed into something memorable. The biblical day of rest is also mandatory for a good stew, curry or soup. Serve it the day you make it and it will be very nice indeed. But wait for it to meld and mellow and it will grow in stature and flavour.

The art of cooking is to know when to leave well enough alone. It can take anything from a few minutes, or half an hour, to a day or two, but you will have executed one of the most crucial techniques in the whole repertoire of cooking. Doing absolutely nothing.

power
& ritual

"I don't care how many diplomas and degrees a kitchen designer has. I want to see his or her collection of cookbooks. Haven't they ever wondered where to put the wok between use?"

■
If you can't stand the kitchen …

When I moved house three years ago, everyone told me how lucky I was. Not only had the whole place been newly renovated, but even the kitchen had been done to a turn. (It was a divorce sale, apparently. Renovating can do that to the best of marriages.)

There it stood, in all its marble and Tasmanian walnut glory, like a double-page spread from *Elle Decoration*, *wallpaper** or *Architectural Digest*. Friends I hadn't seen for a decade were suddenly standing in my kitchen, making that shrill whistling sound between their teeth that I think means wow-that-must-have-cost-a-bomb.

'Grab yourself a mineral water,' I would say smugly, and wait as they would turn, bewildered, looking for the big, white, ugly refrigerator. Hah. Then I would step up to the knotted walnut, tug a discreet black knob, and reveal the designer fridge inside. Next to it, the designer freezer, discreetly clad. Next to it, the designer dishwasher.

Each time, they would cry with delight and shriek with envy. Yep. Everybody loved my kitchen, except the person who had to cook in it. Me.

It didn't take too long to realise that what I had inherited was a kitchen made for looking, not cooking. The fashionable matte black interiors of the cupboards are wonderfully deep, and horrifyingly dark. If I want to cook anything after nightfall—like an evening meal— I have to get in there with a torch. It takes me ten minutes to find the bloody mustard. The designer dishwasher is a dream—until I turn it on and the vibration makes the designer door fall off.

I'm at a loss to understand how a renovation budget that can take in European appliances, recessed spotlights, French doors, hand-made parquetry and a very advanced reverse-osmosis water purifier could stop short when it came to the single sink. Once you have lived with a double sink, there's no going back. It's like getting used to a bidet.

Then there is the whizz-bang dual exhaust filter assembly thingie on either side of the European cooktop that is designed to pull fumes, smoke and steam out of the house, via a large duct. It's ingenious. There's just one thing. It doesn't actually do what it's meant to do. The first time I grilled a steak, the house filled up with smoke, and the neighbours knocked on the door to see if I was all right.

The problem seems to be that kitchens are designed by people who don't cook. I don't care how many diplomas and degrees a kitchen designer has. I want to see his or her collection of cookbooks. Haven't they ever wondered where to put the wok between use, or why so many ovens are installed under the bench, so that the open oven door stops traffic and grazes shins?

So, here's my free, no-obligation consultation to budding kitchen designers everywhere. A kitchen is a living, working part of the house, not just a food-preparation area. Space and natural light are the two top priorities, but are not always available, so at least give us the illusion of both. It needs a really good sound system, with in-built speakers, and as large a table as possible. If there is no room for a table, then put in a high bench-cum-noodle-bar (so much more now than a breakfast bar) with high stools, or a couch and coffee table for lounging.

The bench height should be adjusted to the height of the main cook of the house, and the appliances chosen with one's cooking style in mind (very hot wok-burner for me, thanks), with a terrific exhaust system that isn't as loud as a reversing truck.

At least the kitchen has helped us arrive at a decision regarding the children we were wondering about having. We can't afford to have children. As beautiful as it is, our 280-litre capacity built-in refrigerator could not cope with the demands of a three-year-old. Nor could we, but the fridge is the real problem. There is no way I can get a bigger one without having to pull the entire kitchen down and start again. And we already know what that does to marriages.

"Given that lily ponds are fast disappearing, it is now more likely that you will drink your tea in the company of ugly strangers in a café next to the video arcade in your local Supa Centre."

Brew ha ha

My Auntie May reckons she discovered the cure for cancer more than thirty years ago. Not only that, but she swore blind that a good cup of tea (dash of milk, two sugars) also made pre-menstrual tension disappear, alleviated the misery of gout, provided instant relief from lower back pain and was the perfect panacea for money worries, tiredness, depression and husbands. It makes you wonder what we did before tea came along.

Actually, we drank beer. Until the eighteenth century, the Western breakfast beverage of choice was ale, and a sensible choice it was, too. There's nothing quite like a long glass of something alcoholic first thing in the morning. As you would expect, there were people who cried foul at the switch, refusing to accept that a pale brown liquid brewed from leaves could be more acceptable than a pale brown liquid brewed from hops.

In 1821 a certain William Cobbett wrote:

The drink, which has come to supply the place of beer, has, in general, been tea. It is notorious that tea has no useful strength in it; that it contains nothing nutritious, that it, besides being good for nothing, has badness in it, because it is well-known to produce want of sleep in many cases, and in all cases to shake and weaken the nerves.

Yes, well, tell that to Auntie May. She would have said that William Cobbett could have done with a nice, strong cuppa.

Tell that to Lu Yu, too, who laid down the instructions for a perfect cuppa in his *Ch'a Ching, Classic of Tea*, written around 800 AD. According to him, water had to be brought from a slow-moving stream and heated in an earthenware vessel over a smokeless fire made from olive pit charcoal. As soon as the water boiled, it had to be poured into a blue and white porcelain cup, then emptied again before more boiled water was added to the required amount of tea leaves. To be absolutely perfect, Lu Yu stipulates that the tea should be drunk in the company of beautiful women in a pavilion next to a lily pond. Given that lily ponds are fast disappearing and that a few compromises must be made to account for the passage of twelve hundred years, it is now more likely that you will drink your tea in the company of ugly strangers in a café next to the video arcade in your local Supa Centre.

The Chinese are more realistic than the Japanese, however, who have managed to turn the simple act of tea drinking into a painfully complicated theatrical ritual that makes Chinese opera seem like an easy-to-follow singalong session.

Everything about the Japanese tea ceremony is guided by strict rules, covering the dimensions of the room in which the tea is served, to the number of people who should be present. Topics of conversation are tightly regulated, and each implement and vessel chosen for its artistic merit. The food accompanying the tea must be served in a certain order, so that the texture, flavour and temperature of every dish can be appreciated.

It's not unlike Auntie May's tea ceremony. The room had to be a spotlessly dusted front parlour reserved for State occasions such as weddings and wakes. The number of guests was determined by how many pink floral cups with the tiny handles were left unbroken. The conversation had to be kept well within the confines of the weather, the climate, the maximum temperature and the long-range forecast. And, yes, the food was served in a certain order — first came the scones, jam and cream, then the chocolate digestives, followed by the madeira cake, so that the texture, flavour and temperature of every dish could be fully appreciated. Tea, of course, flowed throughout, in a health-giving, disease-numbing stream.

Mind you, she did eventually die, so it can't be that good for you.

"What is it that these temperamental, moody, headstrong or just plain bloody-minded restaurateurs hate about us? What do we do that is so infuriating that can push them to show us the door?"

How to get thrown out of a restaurant

The first time I was thrown out of a restaurant, I had merely asked the owner if he had any cheeses that weren't pasteurised. My table and I were abruptly parted.

The second time, I asked if the warmish beer I had ordered could be chilled, or replaced with one that was colder. The maître d' arrived at my table and coolly advised me that if I didn't like the temperature at which the fridges had been set, then I should vacate the premises immediately.

In both cases, the response from the restaurateur was a little like passing a sentence of death by lethal injection for parking in a No Standing zone.

The great French chef, Fernand Point at Pyramide in Vienne, was more subtle. When a diner once lit a cigarette immediately after his appetiser, Point promptly presented him with his bill. Similarly, Britain's Nico Ladenis once answered a potential diner's request to bring his own wine with an invitation to bring his own waiters and food as well. In an entire chapter in his book *My Gastronomy*, the opinionated restaurateur–chef challenges the myth that the customer is always right, claiming the revolution in eating habits had left some restaurants generations ahead of their customers.

Marco Pierre White put it down in black and white in his first and never-bettered cookbook *White Heat*: 'If I came to your house for dinner an hour late,' he wrote, 'then criticised all your furniture, and your wife's haircut and said all your opinions were stupid, how would you feel?'

But what is it that these temperamental, moody, headstrong or just plain bloody-minded restaurateurs hate about us? What do we do that is so infuriating that it can push them into such inhospitable rudeness as to show us the door?

An American magazine once surveyed a group of prominent restaurateurs about the things that most annoyed them about their customers. All the usual suspects came up, including no-shows (those who book a table, and then don't turn up), people who want eight different bills for a table of eight, and people who insist on putting their meal together from the components of three or four different dishes.

Right up there with these hardened dining criminals are people who carry their drinks from the bar to the table, people who stand up at the table to greet friends or colleagues, and people who lean across the reception desk and point to their names in the reservations book. I confess to this last crime, if only in an effort to prove I have made a booking under the misspelt name of Mr Durkack, Dorrock, Bewrack or Durex.

If you really want to test the patience of a restaurateur, you can always hang your coat over the back of your chair, help yourself to wine from the ice bucket, click your fingers to attract a waiter's attention and wander from table to table greeting acquaintances. Better still, stay where you are and yell at them from your seat.

Then you can leave your mobile phone next to the pepper grinder, put your make-up on at the table or ask what's special. Or tell the wine waiter every single little detail you know about the wine you've just ordered, ask to have your 'rare only' fillet steak charred to a crisp and leave a cash tip under your plate.

It can't be long before restaurateurs take a leaf out of soccer's book, and introduce a new card or two to their usual rack of Diners Club, Visa, Mastercard and American Express. When you forget yourself enough to do something a little silly, the waiter holds up a yellow card. When you do something seriously unacceptable, out comes a red card, and you're out of there.

It's not ideal, but there seems to be no other solution. Unless, of course, restaurateurs start treating us as if we were guests in their homes, and we behave accordingly.

"These are folk who can calmly look Mother Nature in the eye, then go to their shed and invent a way to undo her that is guaranteed to work to your complete satisfaction in thirty days, or your money back."

■
What does this button do?

used to think the electric toothbrush was really something, until I laid eyes on my very first battery-operated flour sifter. Excitedly, I flicked the switch and felt the power surge into my hand. A pall of flour dust swept over the kitchen bench like a desert scene from *The English Patient*.

How empty, pointless and lacking in meaning my life had seemed up until that very moment. There I was, sifting flour without moving a muscle. No more exhausting squeezing of levers, turning of knobs, or shaking of strainers. While a professional chef needed a battery of utensils to do the job, all I needed was a battery. Here was proof positive that, properly harnessed, natural human ingenuity and inventiveness could triumph over nature and adversity and make this world a better place in which to live.

The scary thing was that my rapture didn't last. It

soon dawned on me that even with an electric flour sifter, my life was still pretty much empty, pointless and lacking in meaning. Then, just as a rabid disbeliever can suddenly embrace the Almighty, I stumbled across the rotary coconut grater. Did I say stumble? Could it not have been pre-ordained? Was it, perhaps, kismet?

Doors opened, pennies dropped and light flooded my dark and dismal existence. I was drunk with the heady power of scraping that pure, tough white flesh from its hairy, hard shell. I grated by day. I grated by night. Little conical towers of grated coconut appeared like ant nests all over the kitchen. I vowed to take up Thai cooking the very next day.

As you may have gathered, I am what is known as gadget-dependent. Cooking for me is not cooking, but an orchestrated blur of bulb-basting, salad-spinning, rotary-whisking, rice-paddling, food-milling, coffee-grinding, vitamising, percolating, fish-scaling, crinkle-cutting, cheese-grating, juicing, ice-crushing, julienning, liqui-dising, frothing, straining and sieving.

I have sharpened cutting and chopping to an artform with my cook's knife, paring knife, filleting knife, carving knife, salmon knife, sushi knife, grapefruit knife, bread knife, chestnut knife, oyster knife and parmesan knife. It's a little embarrassing, but I also admit to owning a croissant cutter, pizza cutter, ravioli cutter, cookie cutter, lattice cutter, nougat cutter, pastry cutter and a very cute radish cutter.

For me, the real heroes in life are the people who

invent these ever more wondrous things. Cracking the macadamia was just that bit ahead of splitting the atom. These are folk who can calmly look Mother Nature in the eye, then go to their shed and invent a way to undo her that is guaranteed to work to your complete satisfaction in thirty days, or your money back.

Nature hides stones in cherries, they invent the cherry pitter. Nature sticks pretty little leaves and stalky bits into strawberries, they create the strawberry huller. Nature grows melons into great big balls, they build implements with scoops on either end that reduce melons to tiny little balls.

The peel on potatoes, the crinkly skin of a pineapple, and the solid armour of oyster and crab shells have all been conquered.

Then of course you have the egg. Awkwardly designed in a brittle shell that won't even stand up on a bench, the egg has only truly been appreciated since the invention of the egg cup, the yolk separator and those natty little scissors that neatly lop the tops off. Next came coddlers, timers, poachers, rings, trees, baskets and the classic, miraculous egg slicer, first manufactured by Bloomfield Industries of Chicago in the 1930s.

We gadget-dependents have been known to evolve. I don't use my butter curler any more, since I started dousing everything with extra-virgin olive oil. I haven't used my meat thermometer for months, since I started stir-frying everything in sight. And I never did get around to using that mushroom peeler, because I never did get around to working out what was wrong with eating mushroom skin.

Some gadgets rise above gadgetdom to become extensions of one's right hand, linked to one's brain: the barbecue tongs, for example, the wire whisk, or the greatest beyond-gadget of them all, the wooden spoon, without which risotto, porridge, custard and everyday living would not be possible.

Even so, if life were a choice between love and a wooden spoon, I'd choose the side of passion and tenderness, with commitment, naturally. If it were a choice between love and a battery-operated flour sifter, however, I'd have to have a serious think about it.

The business of lunch

There they sit, as if they haven't risen from their polished mahogany dining chairs in years. In a way, they haven't.

The cholestorolosaurus, bloated and bullish in a Rumpole-ish sort of way, dressed in what was once a nice piece of chalk-striped handiwork, is making low, guttural sounds, an elbow propped on the white-clothed table, an eyebrow cocked for effect. Reaching the punchline of his story, he thumps a fist down onto the table, rattling glasses. His head is thrown suddenly back with the sheer force of his own thunderous laugh. Haw, haw, haw. Rewarding himself for being so witty, he picks up his glass of claret and drinks deeply.

The prostatosaurus, resplendent in blue blazer with gold buttons, guffaws and shakes his head in helpless mirth, as he spears the enormous lump of charred red meat on his plate. He rips it apart, piles on a few French

"There was always something innately sinister about the idea of big, fat, red-faced men getting another bunch of big, fat, red-faced men pissed on port in order to get a yes instead of a no."

fries, and shovels the lot into his mouth, his sides still heaving like party jelly.

While there are still a few watering holes that attract the odd dinosaur, the business lunch is not what it used to be. This is a good thing.

There was always something innately sinister about the idea of big, fat, red-faced men getting another bunch of big, fat, red-faced men pissed on port, in order to get a yes instead of a no.

The answer is not to kill off the business lunch, but to reinvent it. There will always be a need for business conversations to continue outside the office, for colleagues to get to know each other better, and for people to simply be people, and not just business executives.

So these days, it's mineral water instead of Scotch, white instead of red, fish instead of beef, and taxis called at 2.15 p.m. instead of close to 5 p.m.

The new business lunch is a great deal more flexible than the old, but then, so is the new business. Extended trading hours, less gender bias, the power of the Internet, the whole global thing and the new home office all impact on how we handle our extra-curricular meals. And when we handle them. Some business people refuse to donate even an hour in the middle of the day to eating and drinking with colleagues, and convert all invitations to a breakfast over squeezed juices and yoghurt. That said, we need a few more good restaurants to open for breakfast, before the new business brunch can really catch on.

The new business lunch cannot be recognised by the old signs of heavy, velvet drapes; dark, hidden nooks and crannies; Victorian carvers; the groaning trolley; and girly waitresses with pert noses.

Instead there are glass walls, airy atriums and smart young staff. The diners whiz in, talk over salmon fishcake and a glass of sauvignon blanc, share a panna cotta, toss back an espresso and go.

You can't talk properly while eating a steak. You can tell dirty jokes and go haw-haw-haw a lot, but you can't actually talk properly. Nor do you want anything that has something perfectly nice and simple at the start of its menu description and then goes on and on like an annual general meeting, to include roasted fennel and gazpacho cream with almond wafers and snow pea shoots and black mustard seeds. You're so busy worrying about black mustard seeds in your teeth that you forget to discuss the company's new strategic thrust.

Instead, you want duck and mushroom risotto, slow-roasted tomatoes on crisp polenta with pancetta, or a good piece of roasted cod with buttered cabbage. Stuff you can eat with a fork—antipasto, salad, pasta—is great for business.

Clever lunchers walk there and back, too, returning to the office feeling refreshed, satisfied and stimulated. In fact, they probably end up fitter, happier and more successful than the martyred colleagues left behind at their desks, working through a ham salad sandwich and a can of diet something.

Who would you most trust to solve the problems of the world—the lunchers or the munchers? If only our world leaders would get together and make a block booking for lunch. If they could but swap the hostility of the conference table for the hospitality of the dining table, who knows what could happen.

So it's all agreed then? World peace as of next Monday? Haw-haw-haw.

"Ever since recipes got into print, they stopped evolving and became tyrannical lists of perfectly measured ingredients and specialist techniques. Every time I add a few capers that aren't listed, I look over my shoulder."

You must
give me the recipe

I've just had a great idea for a recipe. You take a pig's trotter, bone it out, stuff it with a mousse of chicken and sweetbreads, and fresh morels. It's brilliant. I haven't been this creative since I invented the upside-down apple tart.

What do you mean it's not original? If someone has done it before, it's nothing but a coincidence. Pierre Koffmann? Really? Well, yes, I probably did glance at his cookbook. But it's still mine.

Legally all I have to do is change the wording, and it's my recipe, not his. So I can take Delia Smith's Thai fishcakes, turn the lime juice into lemon juice and the green chilli into red, and call it Terry Durack's fishcakes. Bingo. People are making Terry Durack's fishcakes throughout the land. Terry Durack is rich and famous. Everyone loves Terry Durack. Except Delia Smith.

But where did Delia get the recipe? There is little to suggest, in a Surrey birth and a Kent childhood, that she inherited Thai fishcakes from her mother. Come to think of it, where do her recipes from? Come to think of it, where do everybody's recipes come from?

They used to come on the sides of flour, cocoa and cereal packets. Before that, they simply existed in the songlines of generations, evolving and devolving through daily demonstration and the spoken word. Ever since recipes got into print, they sort of stopped evolving and became tyrannical lists of perfectly measured ingredients and specialist techniques. Every time I add three tomatoes instead of four, cut the sugar by half or add a few capers that aren't listed, I look over my shoulder to check that nobody is watching. The guilt is tremendous. One food magazine actually warns readers against changing a single measurement or degree of temperature. You're just not allowed.

We can all cook a few things from memory, but how good are we at flying solo on a new dish without the safety net of a cookbook? Let's assume you have already done sausages and mash twice this week, and you have a few chicken pieces in the fridge.

Sure, you can look up 'chicken' in that cookbook you were given for Christmas. It's likely to say poulet Bresse poché-grillé with sauce foie gras (Gordon Ramsay's *Passion for Flavour*), or chicken baked with quince paste and prosciutto (*Marie Claire Food Fast*). Or chicken curry with broccoli and sticky rice (*Gotham Bar and Grill Cookbook*). But what if you don't feel like any of those tonight? Besides, you're running a bit low on foie gras.

There is an alternative, and that is the original, do-it-yourself, no-looking-things-up dinner. Now is the time to create your own recipe as you go.

Come on, you can do it. Just toss some olive oil or butter or both in a frying pan and brown the chicken pieces. Look in the crisper. Oops, nothing. Then look in the pantry, and the freezer. Bung in a can of tomatoes, some saffron and maybe some frozen peas, and simmer gently for one hour, and you've done it. Made dinner! On your own! Not only that, you have come up with an original (insert your name here) recipe.

This is not to say that you can't follow a recipe if you want. I might look up twenty different recipes for osso buco before I start thinking about cooking it. So whose recipe do I end up using? Mine, via Marcella Hazan, Francesco Ghedini, Ada Boni, Antonio Carluccio, Giuliano Bugialli and Valentina Harris. Theirs are the paths along which I tread, but they are not the destination. Nor are there any Mr Ossos or Mr Bucos to thank — just Italy, a million cows and evolution. Some recipes simply belong to the collective kitchens of the world.

But do be careful. When someone asks you where you found the recipe for your fabulous chicken, tomato and peas, they don't like it when you say it's yours. They think you're really up yourself. Such independence also tends to upset people who make a living writing cookbooks, in the same way that happiness and serenity are anathema to those who write self-help books. Besides, if it's any good at all, the bastards will pinch it.

"A boiled egg is not merely an egg that has been boiled. It is a self-contained package, an irresistible alliance of violence and nursery rhymes. To get into it, you must destroy it."

■ Boiling point

The Russian coulibiac of herbed crepes wrapped around a whole salmon with mushrooms and shallots and enveloped in a light brioche dough was a breeze. Preparing the mighty Cassoulet de Castelnaudary with its haricot beans, pork hock, pork ribs, shoulder of mutton, pork rinds, garlic sausage, preserved goose liver and goose confit only took three days.

Even Beijing's famous Dragon and Phoenix, a ten-plate Imperial banquet dish of finely cut meats, vegetables and fish presented in shapes representing dragons, birds, crabs and Chinese characters no longer holds any terror for me, although I'm not sure I'll be doing it again.

The thing that really scares me silly, however, is boiling an egg. There is no room for error in boiling an egg; no margin for creativity or whim, and no place to hide if it is less than perfect. Just the plain boiled fact of how one likes one's egg done—for me, it's with a firm white, and runny in the centre — and how to achieve it.

A boiled egg, you see, is not merely an egg that has been boiled. It is a self-contained package, an irresistible alliance of violence and nursery rhymes. To get into it, you must destroy it. Once broken, it reveals contrasting colours, like a setting sun on the shimmering white surface of a distant planet, and contrasting textures of caramel cream and gummy, molten ooze.

Such a serious matter as boiling an egg deserves serious deliberation, so I consult my favourite food writer, the late M.F.K Fisher. In her treatise, 'How Not to Boil an Egg', she gives two main ways of soft boiling. In the first, she runs the egg under cold water to prevent cracking, then places it gently into simmering, not boiling, water. In the second, she covers an egg with cold water in a little pan. When the water begins to bubble, the egg is done.

In need of another opinion, I retreat to Mrs David, and discover she, too, did far too much research. In *French Provincial Cooking* she gives no fewer than five different ways to boil an egg.

Every damn book I pick up reveals yet another sure-fire hint designed to produce the perfect boiled egg. One insists I stir the water during boiling to centre the yolk within the egg. Another tells me to make a pin hole in the egg to prevent leaks and cracks (tell that to my grandmother). Yet another says to salt the water, which will firm any egg white if the shell happens to spring a leak.

Cooking times vary from author to author, according to their attitude. They also vary according to their altitude, as water will boil at a lower temperature, and therefore take longer to cook an egg, the higher you go. Newly laid eggs will need a minute more than eggs that have been around a while. And so it goes.

Well, it took about five years, but I have now perfected my own method. For one perfect boiled egg, I place two 60-gram eggs at room temperature in a black enamel German Silit saucepan of 18 centimetre diameter. I cover them with 1.25 litres of hot tap water and place the pan over a high gas flame on a Gaggenau stove top, while I sip a cup of tea (Darjeeling). When the water comes to the boil, I reduce it to a gentle simmer and cook the eggs, uncovered, for 3 minutes and 50 seconds. At this point, the white should be set, but still have the slightest tremble about it, and the yolk should have a flowing heart that is just starting to set around its circumference.

I say should, because sometimes it doesn't happen that way. Sometimes my boiled egg saucepan is in the dishwasher, or the eggs vary in weight or temperature, or I'm in a bad mood, or I'm standing on top of a mountain. Then I give the second egg another 30 seconds, and try it. If it's no good either, I give up and just toss together a quick Bombe Alhambra of Italian meringue, strawberry purée and whipped cream, lined with home-made vanilla-bean ice-cream and topped with strawberries marinated in Kirsch. It's so much easier.

"The power of the booth surely goes right back to our childhood playpens. They, too, were easy to get into, and hard to get out of. Nice people kept coming up to you, bringing you food."

The booth, the whole booth and nothing but the booth

Are you or are you not booth-worthy? It's one of the big questions of modern dining. I watched one night as Abel, the mischievous maître d' of London's Atlantic Bar & Grill, was bombarded on all sides by people desperate for a booth.

He had a great system. Anyone who asked for a booth was put at a Siberian table. Anyone young, gorgeous, skinny and, excuse me, but silly enough to not know how to spell booth was given one. Hee-hee. Restaurants may look like the very pillars of capitalist society, but they run on socialist ideals.

The booth, of course, is an inherently socialist ideal in itself. There can be no head of the table, nor anyone below the salt. Everyone in the booth owns and controls an equal amount of space and status. Not only that, but everybody gets to see, and be seen. That's why booths are so desirable, and why they are so glamorous.

Early booths, in tea rooms and pie 'n mash palaces were not so glamorous, but when the booth met Hollywood in the 1940s, the sparks really started flying. No great star had to read the fan magazines or listen to their agent to find out how great they really were. All they had to do was try to get a booth at the Brown Derby, La Rue, The Players or Romanoff's. Especially Romanoff's. This joint was so popular that at lunchtime, the five prized 'A' booths across from the bar were all permanently booked. The first was reserved by Humphrey Bogart, the second by William Morris agent Abe Lastfogel, the third by Louis B. Mayer, the fourth by Darryl Zanuck and the fifth by Harry Cohn.

Booths allowed Hollywood photographers free access to the best sides of the stars—their public faces. Moviegoers were fed a steady diet of glamorous studio-approved publicity shots like the one of Bogart and Bacall with pals John Garfield and Peter Lorre all cosily snuggled up in the padded, studded, rich gold leather booth at La Rue. If they weren't there, they were pictured in a convertible sports car—and what is that but a booth on wheels?

It was the Brown Derby that gave birth to that delicious Hollywood habit—now sadly ruined by the upwardly mobile telephone—of delivering telephones to the table to either take or make a call. It was the solution to a problem: the very act of getting out of a booth could be extremely difficult after three Gibsons and a Manhattan. (Two more Manhattans and it was a piece of cake—one simply slid.)

Eating breakfast one morning in the dining room of the Beverly Hills Hotel, I soon discovered that I was the only one there to eat breakfast. One apparently went there to talk on the telephone. In the next booth, Zsa Zsa Gabor was having a heart-to-heart with her agent. Across the way, a familiar-looking elderly gentlemen had the telephone brought to him no fewer than five times.

I surreptitiously asked the busboy who he was.

'Oh he's, um, er, very famous after the war,' came the enthusiastic reply. 'Great actor'. He was then called to procure another telephone for whatsisface, and swept away. Not to be outdone, I called for a telephone to my booth. It came promptly, and I calmly and efficiently made the call. The time at that very moment was eighten-ten and thirty seconds, precisely.

Like most people, I love a good booth. It makes me feel secure. The power of the booth surely goes right back to our childhood playpens. They, too, were easy to get into, and hard to get out of. After the first month in which you explored the territory and navigated your way around to discover it had four walls, you could relax and feel safe and protected, while still being aware of the world around you.

Besides, nice people kept coming up to you, bringing you food, smiling a lot and making soft, soothing sounds that had a pleasant, calming effect. So today, the booth is our playpen, the closest thing grown-ups have to a demilitarised zone, a place we can call our own, a private world in a public space. And you thought getting a table was difficult.

"We may know that when the recipe tells us to reduce the liquid by half we don't tip half of it down the sink, but sometimes, professional cooking can be a completely foreign language."

A recipe for disaster

I t feels like the start of a beautiful relationship. You know it is going to be risky, but it doesn't matter. Somehow, it just seems right. So you give yourself over to it, and live for the moment. But then things start to fall apart. Literally.

Suddenly, everything you do is wrong. Your confidence sinks, and frustration and anger begin to set in. You blame yourself. You are the one who got it wrong. You are the one who turned something beautiful into ashes. It's not them. It's you.

But wait. Maybe it's not you. In that precious unspoken contract between you and your recipe, maybe—this time—it's the recipe that is at fault. In which case, it is your fault anyway, for investing it with such awesome powers.

If something is printed on paper, has a nice neat list of ingredients, and says it serves four to six people, suddenly it's infallible. Let me tell you, nothing is infallible. When they say something is foolproof, I say hello. I am proof that fools are alive and well.

Sometimes it's an honest or a careless mistake, like the top-selling American cookbook author who published a chicken recipe that unfortunately failed to include chicken in the ingredients. Computers were blamed. Books were reprinted. Countless chickens were saved.

Then there was the foodie magazine recipe for black olive frittata that contained no reference in the ingredients to either eggs or olives.

Sometimes, it's because nobody has actually bothered to test the recipe in the first place, but this is now rare. Authors have to sign a clause in their contract to say that their recipes won't kill anyone, or words to that effect. Ah, but proofreaders don't.

Then there is deliberate sabotage. Yes, in the seamy underbelly of international cuisine, people steal each other's recipes, and protect their own from the possibility of reproduction—even when it is published in a cookbook. I'm not naming names, but the Troisgros Brothers' terrine of vegetables 'd'Olympe' was a bugger of a thing to cook. Maybe it was supposed to fall apart when you cut it. In the end I chucked out the ham and just did chicken for the farce and called it Terrine de Limp instead. Or perhaps it was me, not them.

Some recipes look short but are in fact long, sending you rushing to page 56 for the sauce recipe, page 125 for the demi-glace, and page 173 for how to butterfly the fish.

It's like one of those pure, minimalist houses: very convincing, until you discover they have three rooms full of things like ironing boards, snow skis and suitcases.

Some give you too much information, and some not enough. I had a particularly bad time once with a recipe for *kao soi* noodles, a Northern Thai dish of chicken curry with crisp, deep-fried egg noodles. Throw egg noodles into hot oil and fry until crisp, said the recipe. So I threw dried egg noodles into hot oil and fried until they were ugly, scratchy, burnt toothpicks. Eventually, I contacted the author, a renowned Thai authority, and asked him what I was doing wrong.

'I can't understand it,' he said. 'As long as the noodles are fresh and not dried, it should work perfectly.'

Fresh? Thanks for telling me.

My wife still has one of her grandmother's handwritten recipe books, a knocked-about old exercise book full of perfect copperplate writing, each recipe attributed to friends far and wide. Just about every page has marks and notations to one side. Where one recipe called for a cup of flour, she has written '2 cups', followed by three exclamation marks. Every recipe comes with its own verdict. Those that didn't work received a rather cross cross. Those that pleased got a big tick. Only very few recipes received the big three-tick award.

Could I suggest that all cookbook publishers hire a team of gun grandmas to tick and cross every new crop of cookbooks? Especially with so many chefs doing their thing on the home range these days. We may know that when the recipe tells us to reduce the liquid by half, we don't tip half of it down the sink, and when it suggests we blanch, we don't go pale at the thought, but sometimes professional cooking can be a completely foreign language.

Luckily, there are recipes written by people you trust, a hard core of professionals who test and taste and help and hold your hand if you need it, and leave you alone if you don't. These are the recipes that don't just fail to fail, but succeed in succeeding beyond your wildest. You're not copping the blame any more, but taking the credit.

It's not them, after all. It's you.

Why are we waiting?

A good waiter once told me the secret of his profession. I leant forward eagerly, anxious to know the profound subtleties of his calling.

'Nice,' he said, with a smile, pouring a little more of my favourite pinot noir. 'A good waiter has to be nice.'

But how to be nice when, night after night, your feet are aching, your car is getting a parking ticket and you're working your butt off, surrounded by people who are eating and drinking and having a good time? At least if you worked in a supermarket, you could be as miserable and aggressive as your customers. If you worked in a bank you could be as suspicious and unsmiling as your clients. Diners, however, demand a certain level of perceived hospitality and friendliness from their chosen restaurant.

So waiters are not allowed to let a quiver of annoyance cross their brows when we want the grilled chicken without the eggplant purée, but with the corn

"Waiters are not allowed to let a quiver of annoyance cross their brows when we want the grilled chicken without the eggplant purée, but with the corn and tomato salsa that comes with the veal."

and tomato salsa that comes with the veal instead. Or when we would prefer the salad with balsamic vinegar instead of raspberry, and the mineral water sparkling, but no ice—no, make that with ice, and a squeeze of lemon.

They are not even allowed to whimper when they return from the back of the kitchen, through the scullery and past the dishwashers to the table with said water, only to find that one of your guests would also like a glass. Would anyone else? No. Not until they return with the next glass.

You can only recognise a good waiter after you have had a bad one. These wretched creatures take many forms. There is the 'It's my first night' waiter to whom everything, from the chef's name to the soup of the day, is a source of mystery and delight.

Next is the 'Hello, I'm Darryl' waiter. Resplendent in dad's black bow tie, too-big white shirt and catering suppliers' black, elastic-waisted waiter's pants, he lands on your table like a goony bird and breathlessly announces that he will be looking after you tonight. Every time anybody orders anything, he nods happily and says 'Good choice'. You may not have a good night, but at least you will have made a new friend.

Then there is the 'I'm not really a waiter' waiter, a breed well documented in Los Angeles, where waiters are in fact actors in search of the perfect role, screenwriters in search of the perfect director and clients in search of the perfect agent. They tend to hold the diner personally responsible for the hiatus in their careers, so beware if you are not a film producer, director or agent. And be even more ware if you are.

The school bully grows up to be the *Mein Kampf* waiter, who transforms into an ogre as he slips on his neat black uniform. At London's long-departed Schmidt's restaurant, I once asked a waiter for a German beer, only to be scared out of my wits as he barked: 'Eat first! Drink later!'

I am particularly fond of the 'Everything is special' waiter, who is determined to go through the evening without giving you a shred of advice you could possibly use. There is also the 'I'm not worthy' waiter, who turns grovelling into an artform, and the 'I've only got two hands' waiter who travels through life in perpetual slow motion. And the 'serfbot', a new breed of low-skilled server on automatic pilot. And the Marcel Marceau waiter, who always manages to look as if he is doing something, without managing to do anything at all.

Little wonder that good waiters stand out. They possess an intrinsic, overwhelming sense of hospitality that immediately puts your needs first, without demeaning themselves. They are there when you need them, and not when you don't. They never ask who's having the fish, because they have made a little table map on their pad when taking your order. They are considerate, helpful, knowledgeable and psychic. They can make you feel well-fed, happy, contented, spoiled, good-looking and intelligent.

So to all those waiters out there expecting a big tip from me, here it is: be nice.

culture
& conduct

"The real flavour of exotic and distant cities is their flavour—like the sashimi of raw blood clam at 6a.m. in Tokyo; the shot glass of snake bile in Taipei; and the flying fox stew in Vanuatu."

The travel bug and other delicacies

Seoul is not the most magical city in the world. The men are aggressive, the traffic is unbelievable and there is an air of corporate despair on the busy streets. All those puns about it being soulless ring true. Then, just as you're about to bring your outward-bound flight forward, you find a place like Chang'on, an elegant, peaceful vegetarian restaurant, tucked away in the back streets of Insadong.

Little birds fly through the air, time slows, traffic roar fades away, and gentle flute music pipes in course after course of wild sesame gruel, acorn jelly and perilla leaf tempura. Suddenly you have arrived. You're in Seoul, the real Seoul, taking it in with every bite. When you look back ten years hence, this is the image you will remember. This, and the perilla leaf tempura.

Not being a temple person, monument fan, cathedral hound, museum stalker or shopaholic, for me, the real flavour of exotic and distant cities is their flavour.

Like the sashimi of raw blood clam taken with warmed sake at 6 a.m. at Tsukiji fish market in Tokyo. The shot glass of snake bile in Snake Alley in Taipei, washed down with a glass of snake blood, as the freshly stripped snake still swung from its pole in front of me. The flying fox stew in Vanuatu, eaten in a local pizzeria while I desperately tried to forget I was eating braised fruit bat. There were the fried scorpions in Beijing, followed by the deer's penis garnished with deep-fried sea horses. And the unforgettable scene in the Au Tor Kor produce market in Bangkok, where I stood and watched with sick fascination as a pet monkey lolled about on a couch watching a soap opera on television, while nibbling a satay stick.

Then there's the downside of travel—the stuff in airports, hotels, trains, planes and automobiles. The reheated pastry things, the bain-maried stir-fried things, and the chemically enhanced crisp salty things, all gobbled down because it either was or will be another sixteen hours from any form of sustenance. And the breakfasts, my god, the breakfasts.

Travel junkies will say you must adapt to the local culture: eat as they eat, sleep as they sleep, and so on. Certainly, when in Paris, I am quite happy to forgo my regular breakfast to feast on croissants and *chocolat liquide*. In Guangzhou, I am even happier to give up toast and jam for a few steamers of delicate pork and prawn dumplings. But I once broke down sufficiently to ask for hot toast in a hotel in Xian in Central China. The very helpful waitress brought a slice of white bread.

'Can you toast it?' I enquired politely.

'This is toast,' she said. 'White toast.'

Just as good food can make a bad experience great, bad food can ruin your day. There I was on a sun-drenched schooner, travelling through the islands of Fiji. Millions would have given right arms to be in my place as I worked on my suntan, watched the dolphins play in the wake, chatted with the locals, and helped the skipper load on empty bottles from the main pickup points. I must have looked as if I had won the lottery. But I was absolutely bloody miserable, because next to me on the sweltering deck was a little plastic ice box that my luxury resort had given me for my journey. They packed sandwiches, fruit and chocolate. Unfortunately, what they didn't pack was ice. So after sitting in forty degree heat for several hours, the cooler had converted to a steamer. My sandwiches melted, my chocolate oozed, my banana was brown. It was another six hours to go through the searing heat before reaching Nadi. When I look back, I don't think of the dolphins or the purity of the blue water. I just think of the soggy sandwiches and get really cross.

It's pathetic, really, but there is no getting away from it. If you travel, you have to eat. If you're a good traveller, you'll eat more than the food. You'll take in a little of the air, the soil, the history and the people at the same time, ready to burp up and remember with awe and affection once you're back home having a nice cup of tea and some toast and jam.

"I have set fire to untold tea towels, grated around six tablespoons' worth of knuckles, and stuck myself with trussing needles, skewers, and on one memorable occasion, an oven thermometer."

Enter at
own risk

I have to get myself a safer, less perilous hobby. Something like bomb defusing, rock-face climbing, skydiving or UN peacekeeping would do. Anything but cooking.

I don't think my heart can stand it any more. Even my medical insurance company is starting to get twitchy, not quite believing that a grown man can consistently manage to cut, carve, fry, splatter, steam and scald his way to crippledom year after year.

You know those kitchen gadgets that are so safe that even kids can use them? Well, just keep them out of the way of adults. What those daytime television commercials should really be saying is: 'It chops! It slices! It shreds! It maims! It handicaps! It really hurts!'

I'm not talking about obvious hazards like cleavers, cooks' knives, saucepans of boiling water, slippery-dip kitchen slicers or deep-fryers. I'm talking about plates, glasses, sinks, spoons, cupboard doors, oven racks and cake tins. I could find a way to do serious damage with one of those rubber spatulas if I were left alone with one long enough.

A case in point was the day I finally cracked it for the perfect taramasalata. I had been working on it for weeks, changing the bread here, increasing the proportion of cod's roe and lemon juice there, and experimenting with a variety of olive oils.

Then, finally, I got it. As it whizzed around in the blender, I could smell that it was perfect, just the right balance of summery spice and tang. It had none of the fluorescent pinkness of more commercial versions, but it looked and smelt great. Then it started to clump.

I turned off the blender, lifted the lid and started breaking it up with my hands. (Please, whatever you're about to say, I've heard it already.) Then my hip pushed the 'on' button at the front of the machine, and for a split second, my kitchen turned into a scene from an 'Itchy and Scratchy' cartoon.

I yanked my hand out, but not before the tarama turned a pretty shade of rose pink. It was then that my wife walked in.

'Wow,' she said. 'Great colour.'

Since then, I have set fire to untold tea towels, grated around six tablespoons' worth of knuckles, stuck myself with trussing needles, skewers, and on one memorable occasion, an oven thermometer.

The most painful dish I have ever made was

Singaporean chilli crab for eight friends. I blame myself, however, and not my new, wobbly wok. Nowhere in the recipe does it say, 'Pour smoking hot oil over your right hand before adding crab'. Fortunately one of my guests was a professional chef, who immediately filled a bucket with ice and water and stuck my still-sizzling right hand in it, thereby adding immeasurably to my life skills. I now know how to eat crab with chopsticks in my left hand.

I know what you're thinking. It's me that's the hazard, and not the kitchen. Only amateurs make mistakes, right? Wrong. I once worked in the kitchen of a very experienced Swiss-trained seafood chef, who had encountered more crabs than another crab would see in a lifetime, in a distinguished career spanning three countries and three decades. Then one day, a careless moment, a loose claw, and wham, twelve stitches in the webbing between thumb and forefinger.

Another well-respected chef of my acquaintance lost both eyebrows and his equilibrium when a small trout-smoking gadget blew up in his face.

Ask any professional chef to pull up his or her sleeves, and you'll see the truth: burn marks, and lots of them, like the gradations on a school ruler. If they're not there, then your chef is obviously an Executive Chef, too highly placed to do the hands on, arms burnt, sort of stuff.

Now, if you don't mind, I think you should stand well back. I'm about to make a ham and cheese sandwich.

"The toast and cornflakes thing is a conditioned response to the threat of change. We cling to the culturally familiar, knowing the unfamiliar awaits us beyond the kitchen door."

The champions
of breakfast

Okay, so you interrupted a naked foie gras orgy on a Nepalese hilltop for what? A dusty piece of white toast and a bowl of soggy cornflakes? Well, of course you're going to be disappointed.

Breakfast is the only meal of the day for which you have to stop dreaming and get out of bed. That's an awfully big load to put on a single nutritional moment. No wonder even the corn flakes under the pressure.

In truth, the average breakfast is simply not up to it. It's just too banal, bland, boring and nutritious. One of life's great puzzles is that while we are only too happy to immerse ourselves in the cultures and food habits of exotic, alien outposts at lunch and dinnertime, we mysteriously revert every morning to the timid and unadventurous creatures we obviously are, physically unable to break the breakfast habits of a lifetime.

It's because we are still in our vulnerable post-snooze

state, with hair as yet unbrushed and mind as yet unsharpened. So the toast-and-cornflakes thing is a conditioned response to the threat of change. We cling to the culturally familiar, knowing the unfamiliar awaits us beyond the kitchen door.

Even when we blow out (on Sundays, or anywhere near room service), we're totally predictable. 'I think I'll live on the edge and have a fried egg, lots of bacon, a big fat pork sausage, oh and hash browns on the side.'

Well, whoopee-doo. We are now at the stage when bacon 'n eggs is a thrill. Mind you, back when Yugoslavia was a country whose name you could pronounce, an associate once ordered the big B & E in a Belgrade hotel dining room. After consulting an undersized bilingual dictionary and an oversized waiter, he was ceremoniously presented with a plate containing a piece of warmed speck (a thick, fatty slab of paprika-spiked smoked pork) and two Russian eggs awash in mayonnaise and dotted with black lumpfish roe.

'Beckon undt ecks,' announced the waiter proudly.

In Barcelona, I clung to the well-shod heels of the great chef Isidre Gironés Escolano as he trawled through the stalls of the famous Mercat de la Boqueria in the wee small hours, marvelling at his ability to combine food marketing with sex. (At that hour. Anyone can do it later in the day.)

The more he flirted with the beautifully aged women behind the meat and fish counters, the lower the prices dropped. Pleased with his haul, Señor Escolano invited me to join him for 'a little breakfast' at his favourite market restaurant, El Turia.

With visions of pretty little sugar-dusted churros and hot chocolate dancing in my head, I sat down as the sun came up — to a banquet of casseroled snails and pigs' trotters; murderously rich, dark, bloody morcilla sausages, and crisp, lemony saltcod fritters. I seem to recall a gloriously gluey bathtub of braised tripe as well; and a bottle or two of soft red local wine (Ylleva) and, finally, coffee corrected with Catalan brandy.

Now I know why Catalans don't eat lunch until the middle of the afternoon. They pass out for eight hours after breakfast.

Then there was a simple little breakfast taken at Jean Georges restaurant at the foot of New York's Trump International Tower and Hotel, a spire of blond and bland accommodation. I dithered, as one does, between the scrambled eggs with caviar and vodka cream, popped back into their cute little shells, for US$21, or the poached eggs with freshly shaved truffles and potato pancakes for US$24, then decided to have both. I found that if you drink enough hot Valrhona chocolate along the way, there's no problem.

So what's for breakfast? Roasted vegetables and aïoli? Blood pudding on toast? Rice pudding and berries? Sweetcorn fritters with roasted tomatoes? Ricotta hot cakes with honeycomb butter? Or miso with pickles?

The only question is how much room you have left, after all that foie gras.

"You grab a dumpling with your chopsticks, pop it in your mouth, and burn the hell out of your tongue as the searingly hot pork and soupy juices explode in a fireball of flavour. You don't do this again."

Planet Dumpling

Dateline Shanghai: it's hot, steamy, and wall-to-wall humanity, as waves of people surge forward, almost dwarfed by the soaring towers. Only I'm not talking about the city. I'm talking about lunch.

It is rush hour in the Nanxiang, Shanghai's most famous dumpling house. Steam pours from the kitchen as if from a Swedish sauna, and waiters on a mission from the kitchen god emerge with trays piled skyscraper high with dark, damp bamboo steamers.

It's not the sort of place your tourist guide will take you, although it is a place to which you should take your tourist guide. The stoic, all-knowing Helen, who can rattle off 500 words on the Shanghai Museum at the drop of a Qing dynasty vase, sits there silent, her eyes stricken and her lips opening and closing like a fish out of water.

She is not to be blamed. I had already bucked the system by refusing to see the giant jade Buddha, on the grounds that it could only be incrementally more boring than looking at a small jade Buddha, and insisted on visiting a real street market. She was beginning to despair that my road to cultural enlightenment was paved with restaurants rather than temples, until I asked her to take me to the Yu Yuan Gardens.

'Aah, the Yu Yuan Gardens,' she exclaimed joyfully. 'Constructed between 1559 and 1577 as the home of the Pan family, rich officials from the Ming Dynasty.' And so it went for the next hour or so, until we emerged from the gardens and I saw my goal.

'Oh look,' I said, eyebrows raised with intellectual curiosity. 'A dumpling house.'

'Oh, yes, that is a quite famous dumpling restaurant,' said Helen. 'Shanghai has a permanent population of fourteen million people, supplemented by a shifting population of three million.'

'Do tell,' I said, bounding up the stairs, trampling a few small children as I weaved through the crowds. Henceforth I became the guide. Helen didn't know the restaurant's name came from the nearby town of Nanxiang, where the *xiaolongbao* (steamed pork dumplings) are said to be juicier, lighter and more succulent than any other in the province.

Nor did she know how to get a table. First you have to go to the counter and wave money at a girl with more tickets than British Rail. Then nominate in whatever language you can muster (fingers work best) how many steamers you want. She then says something like 'You want ginger with that?' Nod, and wave more money, and maybe point to the Tsing Tao beer in the nearby glass-doored fridge. She will issue you with pink, white and blue tickets that mean nothing to you. Grasp them firmly, for they are your admission to heaven. Then go and stand behind a nice family calmly eating their dumplings at one of the twelve dark wooden tables. You can always try glaring at them to make them feel uncomfortable and they will leave faster.

Immediately claim their chairs as your own and slap your tickets down on the table. Eventually, huge damp steamers will arrive, each bearing a necklace of neatly pinched pale white purses that smell sweet and pure.

You grab one with your issued chopsticks, pop it in your mouth and burn the hell out of your tongue as the searingly hot pork and soupy juices explode in a fireball of flavour.

You don't do this again. You learn respect. You learn to wait. You learn to plunge your tongue into your beer. You learn, finally, how to eat *xiaolongbao*.

One. Talk among yourselves as they cool a little. Pour red vinegar from the teapot (yes, the teapot) on the table over your little dish of shredded ginger.

Two. Lift a dumpling to your mouth, purse your lips. Simultaneously bite a hole in the pastry and suck out the hot broth.

Three. Dip your dumpling in the vinegar, allowing a little to seep in through the hole.

Four. Eat. Chew slowly and resolutely. Wait for the

slow, satisfied smile to creep across your face.

Five. Go for another.

Six. Go for another. Et cetera.

I ate sixteen. So did Helen. With two beers, the ubiquitous Sprite, plus ginger, it cost about as much as two cups of coffee in my local café. Afterwards, I was happy and content, but my guide looked forlorn. When pressed, she shook her head sadly. 'I fear you are not learning anything about Shanghai.'

To the
manners born

I t's time we rounded up all the kids and the trouble-makers and took away their knives. I'm serious. It's too dangerous. I'd take away their forks and spoons as well, if I could, and I wouldn't give them back until they promised to use them properly.

The generation that is computer-literate by the age of seven seems unable to grasp the concept of eating with a knife and fork. Perhaps it is because it no longer uses an elegant writing tool such as a pen, that it feels a deep, subconscious urge to hold a knife in the same manner, carving graffiti-like swathes across the plate. Or perhaps it is because it has less need for knives. Home-delivered pizzas and deep-fried potato chips do not require cutting and dividing into small portions.

Now that Grandma is in a home and not at the dinner table, there is nobody around long enough to nag some table graces into our heirs. So now we have kids who

"Now that Grandma is in a home and not at the dinner table, there is nobody around long enough to nag some table graces into our heirs."

hold their knives and forks as if they are drumsticks, Nintendo controls, motorcycle handles or guitar picks. It's the sign of a deeper tragedy: that a code of ethics once known as table manners has gone the way of— well—the table.

I wouldn't be surprised to learn that it is the same the world over. That mothers and fathers in the Pacific Islands constantly nag their children for not having the common decency to burp after dinner, and that Japanese mums have given up hope that their offspring will stop eating their noodles silently, and start slurping them loudly like normal, civilised human beings. Or that Moroccan dads go around praying for the days their sons will finally learn to eat with their hands like grown-ups. Or that Turkish kids are getting into hot water for not spilling a single drop of their tea into the saucer, when everyone knows that an overflowing cup is a sign of a generous spirit and a proper upbringing.

The table manners of the last generation simply lose their relevance to the next. Who among us would now heed American taste arbiter Emily Post's dictum that elbows can only be on the table if one is ill or alone?

We need to codify new forms of acceptable behaviour that are relevant to the new ways in which we eat, and lose those stultifying rules that preserve only pretension. Even an Emily Post-Modern would have to agree that the fish knife is a ridiculous folly, a useless, blunt instrument that can only succeed in torturing a decently cooked fish.

We need to be told if it is polite to scoop the fluff from

a cappuccino before drinking, and what not to do with one's chopsticks. We should probably be guided into the dunking etiquette of focaccia when it concerns a communal bowl of olive oil, and, more crucially, of the potentially serious social offence of double-dipping, the Seinfeldian act of dipping one's corn chip not once, but twice, into the party bowl.

(The answers, in order: Yes, but don't leave the spoon in your mouth longer than five seconds. Never leave chopsticks sticking out of your food or rice bowl. Yes, but only once, or pour a little of the oil from the bowl onto your own bread and 'butter' plate and dip from there. And finally, nothing is more serious than double-dipping. Not even parking your handbag on the table while you eat.)

It takes a certain maturity, shall we say, to realise that while manners do not maketh the man, they do maketh life that much easier. They are important not so much in their own right but for what they represent. Not in terms of depicting one's social standing, but in their silent demand that we take the time to treat each other with small kindnesses, a little consideration and some respect; that we put our dining companions ahead of ourselves.

Manners are all that separate the act of eating from the art of dining. So would you mind sitting up straight and not rocking back on your chair while I'm talking to you?

Ten green
bottles

I t seems a rather bizarre admission to make, but I once
bought an alcoholic beverage solely because of its
colour. This total lapse in commonsense occurred
during my Swinging Sophisticated Cocktail Set period,
when I was liberally experimenting with mind-altering
substances. They came in a psychedelic palette of colours
including electric blue (Blue Curacao), bright yellow
(Chartreuse), emerald green (crème de menthe), and one
particularly over-the-top number with gold flecks sus-
pended in it, like a drinkable snow dome. (Hands up
everyone with a bottle of Goldwasser in the back of the
cupboard. Okay, hands down, somebody might see you.)

Buying Blue Curacao is one thing. Trying to find
something sensible to do with it is another matter alto-
gether. It is remotely possible that the Luisita (Blue
Curacao, barley water, lemon juice and soda), winner of
the 1966 Italian National cocktail competition, wasn't

"The only thing
I can say in my
defence is that I
can't remember a
single thing. As
anyone who has ever
tasted a grasshopper
will know, this is
not necessarily a
bad thing."

totally terrible. A Blue Devil (gin, lime, Maraschino and Blue Curacao) has at least the advantage of using up both the Blue Curacao and the Maraschino. Most of my concoctions, however, tasted an awful lot like a blue rinse gone wrong.

But things improved. Soon after this period, I flew into Bangkok jet-lagged to (and from) the high heavens, and checked into The Oriental Bangkok. Well, actually, I checked into the cocktail lounge, where it happened to be happy hour.

The next thing I knew, it was three o'clock the following afternoon, and I was in bed with my clothes on. Hmmm. I showered, dressed, and dropped into the bar for a pre-dinner drink.

'Ah, Mr Grasshopper,' beamed the cheerful barman.

'I'm sorry?' I said. Obviously he had mistaken me for someone else.

'You like another grasshopper, Mr Grasshopper?'

'Look,' I said firmly, 'I don't even like crème de menthe.' Suddenly there was a wide-mouthed martini glass of white-and-green crème de menthe and cream frothing by my hand.

'There,' he announced triumphantly, 'the usual.'

The only thing I can say in my defence is that I can't remember a single thing. As anyone who has ever tasted a grasshopper will know, this is not necessarily a bad thing.

Many of us have these bottles lurking in the backs of cupboards to this day. They get pushed to the rear as we invest in their less flamboyant modern equivalents. Blue is now the more subtle hue of Bombay Sapphire Gin; green is now Midori melon liqueur; while yellow is the southern Italian Limoncello. But for those rumbling through the cupboard in search of a little cheer, only to unearth a vomitous rainbow of green, red, orange and purple stuff, salvation is at hand.

Sake, for example, can be employed in a rather gorgeous little concoction known in New York as the saketini (three parts frozen sake, one part dry vermouth, shake and strain, twist of lime peel).

If there is any Pimm's No. 1 Cup lying around (and of course there is), congratulations. It's fabulous in a VIP (gin, Pimms, passionfruit juice, dry vermouth and lemon juice), created by barman John Doxat for a Taylor and Burton film of the same name. Even crème de menthe can take on social credibility when transformed into a Caruso (one part dry gin, one part dry vermouth, one part crème de menthe, shake over crushed ice). As for Blue Curacao, sorry, but you're on your own.

If you still have a few liqueur bottles left, you have no taste, less shame and don't mind a little cheap exhibitionism, then the ultimate cupboard-cleaner-outerer is a *pousse-café*, an amusing construction consisting of separate layers of differently coloured and weighted liqueurs.

Or you could give up and serve vodka. After all, it's the spirit of the third millennium. It's colourless, odourless and tasteless. But I ask you, is it as much fun?

Bum raps

'This chair's too small.'
  'This one's too big.'
  'This one's too hard.'
Serial diners are just like Goldilocks, always looking for the restaurant chair that's juuuuust right. The dining chair, after all, is the very foundation of the dining experience. It's the bottom line, representing that crucial point where the designer meets the diner.

Get a bad chair, and chances are you won't notice it. You won't stay long, either. No extra-curricular dessert wine or coffee and petits four for me, thanks, early morning, you know how it is. Get a good chair, however—and you still won't notice it, right through three courses, coffee and far too many cognacs.

You can tell how long you are meant to stay in a restaurant by the nature of its chair. The hard benches of the noodle bar are designed to send you on your way as

"If the Australian chair were a person, it would be a Swedish back-packer on Bondi Beach: always tanned, blond and wooden, and happier out on the terrace in the sun than cooped up in a dining room."

quickly as possible, to make room for the next lot of faithful slurpers. Few noodle bars make their money from the cognac and liqueur list.

A warm, comfy, padded armchair, on the other hand, says welcome, chief executive officer; settle in, lord of the realm; and make yourself at home, ruler of the universe. We are but your slaves.

A great chair works with your body, and not against it. It is in proportion with the table, and in harmony with its surroundings. It's not so high that your feet are left dangling off the floor, and not so low that you feel you are a five-year-old at the grown-ups' table. It doesn't wobble, scrape the floor with a screech, or make your bum go numb.

Some chairs try too hard. You don't know whether to sit in them, or to stand in front of them wondering aloud what the artist was really trying to say. Some look like the thing you took home from school after Metalwork 101, others look like *Apollo 13* crash pads. Then there is the garden furniture that has escaped the great outdoors in order to ruin the great indoors. Unless your dining room is prone to extremes in temperature and the occasional downpour, I can't see the point.

Some chairs wrap themselves around you like a sumo wrestler's bear hug. They tend to get up to go to the bathroom at the same time as you do. Then there is the designer bum rap: all angles and curves, over-garnished and under-ergonomical. I recall one such chair that, rather than being shaped to one's posterior, actually rose in the middle of the seat in an attempt to divide and conquer. Gave me quite a fright at the time.

If you are looking for the very essence of a nation's character, the answer is right under its collective bottom. A French chair has character, poise, confidence. It stands more seriously at the table, with a sense of purpose, waiting for that soft, powdered derrière, for the tap of high heels on old parquetry, secure in the knowledge of its birthright. A traditional British chair is as much at home in the drawing room as the dining room. All polished wood and glowing velvet, it is designed to impress rather than be impressed upon.

But oh, those Spanish chairs. Clean, curvaceous lines, long, lean legs, and a flash of humour—I could sit there all night. American chairs? Well, think airport, think commercially viable, think capable of carrying the weight of a fully grown corn-fed steer.

If the Australian chair were a person, it would be a Swedish back-packer on Bondi Beach: always tanned, blond and wooden, and happier out on the terrace in the sun than cooped up in a dining room.

The truly great chairs do not come along every day. Michael Thonet invented the classic Vienna bentwood chair in 1859, which went on to become the biggest-selling chair of all time. Arne Jacobsen invented the revolutionary ant chair in 1955, made from nine layers of wood that were steamed, moulded then glued together. You may or may not remember that one-time British good-time gal Christine Keeler added considerably to its popularity by being photographed naked and astride, thereby succeeding in confusing many as to the correct way to be seated.

What's next? The cube. My local sandwich shop simply has cubes on wheels that can be moved to form tables, chairs and magazine stands. No legs, no backs, no arms, no scraping, no wobbling and no designer features, because it is in itself a designer feature. That should make everyone happy—except that pain in the bum, Goldilocks.

"On a friend's recommendation I once ended up eating raw garlic and acidic tomato purée in Italy, when it dawned on me that this was exactly the kind of restaurant he liked to eat in back home."

Civilisation: a survival guide

Every generation has its own survival guide. My esteemed father-in-law, an ex-air force squadron leader, has given me his: a remarkable pocket-sized book entitled *Jungle, Desert, Arctic & Ocean Survival*, published during World War II.

In it is advice on when to bail out of your plane, how to make snow goggles from a piece of wood, and how to trap a monkey. There is a very handy crash course on speaking Eskimo. 'Comma-tee-nick eye-shook-too' means bring a dog sled. We hope.

It is particularly informative on what you can and can't eat. You can't eat polar bear livers, jellyfish, parsnip root and sea snakes. You can eat termites (having carefully removed the wings), beetle grubs, ground ferns, musk ox and seals. The author even reveals a distinct penchant for caribou brisket.

This is all very well, but what this generation needs is

a survival guide for when you're stranded in the middle of civilisation. One of the great problems facing the modern traveller is finding a decent restaurant in a strange city. You already know enough not to go to the first restaurant to the right of your hotel, anywhere with touts at the door, or any place that advertises in the free tourist magazine in your room.

You also know enough never to eat in your hotel, unless you happen to be staying at the Cipriani in Venice, the Peninsula in Hong Kong or the Hotel de Paris in Monaco, home to Ducasse's Le Louis XV restaurant.

And I don't need to remind you about taxi drivers, do I? By all means entrust your suitcase to them, but not your stomach. Thanks to taxi drivers, I have discovered the worst *smorrebrod* in Copenhagen, the worst roast beef (I think it was beef) in Scotland and the worst meat pie in Sydney.

Instead, I have developed my own methods. How else would I have found the Lung Wah pigeon restaurant in Hong Kong or the magical Cave di Maiano rooted by grapevines to the steep Florentine hills?

I find most of my great restaurants in other great restaurants, by grilling the waiter. All over the world, the restaurant industry is so close knit, it's almost incestuous. Almost everyone knows who has moved where, who's just opened there, and who's sleeping with whom.

After a single meal at Jeremiah Tower's glamorous Stars Brasserie in San Francisco, I gleaned enough to keep me well fed for a month—at the mighty Swan Oyster

Depot, the evergreen wood-fired Zuni's, and the roast-chicken-and-beer Lulu.

But surely you just buy the local restaurant guide, I can hear you cry. Maybe so, maybe not. Does it take ads? Are the reviews written by A. G. Lutton, pseudonym of the guy who sells the ads? Even honest guides like the virtuous *Guide Michelin* can land you with a platter of *loup de mer à la crème* faster than you can say 'Do we have enough to pay for this?' And inevitably, by the time you arrive at your 'typical friendly little Roman trattoria', it is filled with Americans and Japanese, the Romans having absconded when it was 'discovered'.

As for the American-based Zagat guides, democratically compiled by thousands of diners, I just worry that many of those thousands are like my friends. On a friend's recommendation I once ended up eating raw garlic and acidic tomato purée in Italy, when it dawned on me that this was exactly the kind of restaurant he liked to eat in back home. How he managed to find one just as bad in Italy was a miracle.

The truth is, you don't need a manual to find a great restaurant when you travel. You just need to do a bit of homework, cross-reference a couple of waiters, and pack a well-developed instinct for self-preservation. In the words of my father-in-law's guide, you will always survive if you get plenty of sleep and rest, avoid tight clothing, keep dry and warm, eat plenty of fat, and stay away from the women. Better advice than that, the *Guide Michelin* could not give you.

"We live in a world where slow-cooked salmon with porcini risotto and black pudding appear on the one plate, and where it's considered acceptable to serve harissa-spiced poussin on Chinese cabbage."

Local heroes

Testaroli is one of the most exciting dishes I have ever eaten. It is both rare and everyday. It tastes very old, yet very avant-garde. It is one-of-a-kind. What do you mean, you haven't heard of it? Of course you haven't heard of it.

To experience *testaroli*, you have to fly to Milan, and catch the train to Genoa. Then you catch another train to La Spezia, the town that marks the southern full stop to the Ligurian coastline known as the Italian Riviera. Now you have to get a local train to the village of Sarzano in the Lunigiana region, which sneaks its way over the border into Tuscany. I would recommend you stop in the square for a coffee and a slice of sweet onion focaccia, to catch your breath.

From here on, you need an uncle who has lived in the area all his life. I immediately adopted Mario Guelfi, who was raised in Sarzano, and now owns the genuinely good

Ciccio seafood restaurant in nearby Bocca di Magro, at the very mouth of the Magro river.

Without an uncle, it will do you no good asking for *testaroli*. They will just look at you strangely, shake their head, and move off. And that's just in Sarzano, its home town. In the next village, they may never have heard of it at all. My new Uncle Mario, however, will take you at breakneck speed up winding roads to his home, where the *testaroli* has been baked in his hand-made oven, fired by olive wood, and tended by the modest, hard-working Uncle Andrea.

Testaroli is a huge flat round pancakey thing made from wholemeal wheat dough. Since Roman times, it has been cooked on hot slate in flat earthenware discs known as *testi*. It bakes until firm, but that is only the first half of the process. It is then cut into bite-sized pieces, and boiled in simmering water as you would cook pasta, until it softens. Uncle Mario then dresses it in the famous Ligurian pesto, made from his sweet, home-grown basil.

What makes *testaroli* even more delicious is the realisation that there is practically nowhere else in the world you can eat it. There are no *testaroli* bars in Venice Beach; and no *testaroli*-to-go corners in our local supermarkets. There is no Testaroli Haven, Planet Testaroli or Testaroli King. You will barely find it in an Italian food reference library. It doesn't rate a single mention in Carluccio's *Italian Food*, and is nowhere to be found in Anna Del Conte's otherwise comprehensive *Gastronomy of Italy*.

We live in a world where slow-cooked salmon with

porcini risotto and black pudding appear on the one plate, and where it's considered acceptable to serve harissa-spiced poussin on Chinese cabbage with a mirin-infused jus.

The most popular restaurant in Shanghai is German. In Taipei, they're all eating Italian pizza. The hottest chefs in Hong Kong are Californians or Australians, while the architects of Singapore's New Asian cuisine are Swiss- and German-trained hotel chefs.

McDonald's now rules in Rome and the queues outside the KFC ('*kendeji jiaxiang ji*') in Beijing are longer than those outside the Qianmen Quanjude Peking Duck restaurant.

So *testaroli* has become a symbol for me, a shield held high against the onset of the global kitchen.

Another weapon in my armory is the memory of Uncle Mario's *farinata*, a flat, chickpea-flour tart flavoured with olive oil and pepper and oven-baked until crisp and golden outside, and meltingly soft inside. Dating from pre-Roman times, it is traditionally cooked in a special wrought-iron baking dish.

The reason so many of these local dishes are not known outside the area is because of the relative isolation of the Ligurian coastline, fringed by the sea, and hemmed in by steep mountain sides. Feeling proud of myself for unearthing one of the last bastions of real regional cooking, I found myself boasting across a table to the New York food critic and author Jeffrey Steingarten, self-billed as the man who ate everything. *Farinata*,

I reckoned, is one thing he would not have eaten.

Wrong. He apparently loved the stuff so much on his last trip to Liguria that he lugged two incredibly heavy *farinata* pans back to America.

Omigod, not America. If *farinata* has reached the States, the *testaroli* burger can't be far off.

■ Feed a fever

I had been throwing up for three days. By now, I had an intimate knowledge of the inner workings not only of my body, but of the small Lyonnaise bathroom in which it was sequestered.

All my longed-for dreams of *la grande bouffe* in Lyons were going down le drain. It had taken me years to get there, and many hours planning meals in the local *bouchons* (bistros) and three-star Michelin restaurants. I had entertained visions of buckets of Beaujolais and tables groaning with fireman's aprons (braised tripe), stuffed pigs' feet and hearty beef daubes.

To set the tone for this gastronomic odyssey, I kicked things off with a visit to a restaurant known for its *andouillettes*, earthy, foul-smelling, divine-tasting sausages made of pigs' intestines.

I wined, I dined, I laughed, I caroused. Then at about 3 a.m., back in bed at my hotel, I writhed, I winced,

"No buckets of Beaujolais and stuffed pig's feet for me any more. Just buckets. Even the thought of a cup of tea was enough to send me running in all directions."

I groaned, I convulsed. No buckets of Beaujolais and stuffed pigs' feet for me any more. Just buckets. Even the thought of a cup of tea was enough to send me running in all directions.

Then, miraculously, on the third day, I rose again, struck by a vaguely familiar pang. Could it be? Yes, it was! Hunger. I went into the first restaurant I could find, an unassuming lunchtime spot called Guillaume Tell. The menu swam before my eyes. Everything was too rich, too creamy, too this or too that. Besides, my hunger was more of the delicate, rug-over-the-knee, help-me-please-kind-sir type. My eyes fixed on the one thing on the menu that I could swallow. *Oeuf en gelée.*

There it was, a single egg encased in a glistening savoury jelly. It's not a good thing to do to an egg, really. A week earlier, I would have called it bland, boring and a waste of good eating time. But my first tentative mouthful was full of flavour, depth and complexity. I missed not a single nuance of the gentle smooth egg white, the lusciousness of the egg yolk, and the hint of tarragon in the aspic.

There are some foods that you can only fully appreciate when you are in a weakened state. Something happens to your tastebuds when you get sick that makes them ultra-sensitive and more receptive to barely-there flavour compounds. Anything more than a glass of milk is enough to blow them away. It's almost as if the palate returns to a natural childhood state, before it became jaded with sophisticated, spiced, adult fare.

Tastebuds get quirky and irritable, too, when the host body gets sick. Mine want lemonade, slightly flat and at room temperature. It's not something I would drink if it were left to me, but they demand it.

A higher fever and a soaring pulse, and they put in an order for chicken soup. If they can handle carrots and celery, I know I'm not that sick. But the more depth of flavour they detect in the broth itself, the more sick I am.

The Italians have a wonderful term for eating invalid food—*mangiare in bianco* or to eat white—referring to the easily digestible, understated dishes that we instinctively return to whenever we're feeling unwell, unloved or just not sure about things. A plain risotto, for instance, spaghetti with a little butter and cheese, or *stracciatella* soup of shredded egg in chicken broth.

Similarly Japan has *chawan mushi*, a pale, delicate, subtle egg custard. China has pale, white-poached chicken, and bowls of congee, thick white rice soup. Greece has scented rice pudding. I'm sure the French have more than *oeuf en gelée*, but I owe my life to that shivery little thing. I have since tried to eat a jellied egg in an effort to revisit that therapeutic experience, only to decide it was bland, boring and a waste of good eating time.

Even Anglo-Saxon culture is rich in white, invalid food. Think mashed potatoes, poached eggs, tapioca, sago pudding, junket and milk jelly.

Milk jelly. That reminds me: feel my forehead. Does that seem hotter than normal to you?

greed
& obsession

"There is no denying the power of the café. It could be the wood panelling, the company, the endearing inevitability of the biscotti, panini and gelati. But it's probably just the caffeine."

The power
of the café

I did a thorough check at the office of births, deaths and marriages, and found nothing.

When I asked the nice young woman at the counter if there couldn't be some mistake with my birth certificate and could she run it through the computer again, she stared at me edgily. She then began fumbling about under the bench for what I could only assume was some sort of panic button for use in situations involving unstable, unbalanced or unreasonable members of the public.

So, in a very reasonable, stable and balanced manner I ran for the door. But I still didn't believe there wasn't a conspiracy going on to hide my real identity. I talked to all my living relations, which did no good at all, and eventually hit the Internet to contact one of those obsessive family tree types who spend their lives chasing family crests. They, too, were very sorry, but could not confirm there was any Italian blood in my veins.

This I cannot believe. Because every time I walk into an Italian café, I feel as if I am coming back home. In a good café, I feel like Mastroianni. After two coffees, the women all look like Isabella Rossellini and Carla Bruni, and I'm in heaven.

My particular problem aside, there is no denying the power of the café. It could be the wood panelling, the intriguing company, the endearing inevitability of the biscotti, panini and gelati. But it's probably just the caffeine. The real engine room of this power is the espresso machine. A café's heart and soul is poured daily into a small porcelain cup, and given over to this cup are hundreds of years of precision, ritual and formality.

There is no point trying to make decent coffee at home, if A, you're not Italian, and B, you're making coffee for one or two, and not three hundred.

I have tried using those ludicrously expensive baby espresso machines. I've even bought one. I've tried the new breed of cheap domestic machines. I've even bought one. But there is little point. We don't have the power, the size or the pressure of the café equivalent, so there's no body, no aroma and no *crema*. Just nice, warm, coffee-flavoured stuff.

Those two precious cups of coffee we finally tweak out of the machine for breakfast would be tossed into the sink at the start of the day in any self-respecting café.

At my local, they turn on *la macchina* at 5.30 a.m. and run twenty to thirty espresso coffees through it to warm it up, while the staff play with the grind and the pressure. These rejects then go into the kitchen to be used in making tiramisu. This is why I never eat tiramisu.

The mecca of mocha for true café lovers is Rome. There looking for long-lost relatives, I decided to concentrate my search in Rome's finest cafés. Obviously, that's where any relative of mine would turn up. I traipsed through Trastevere, veered into the Via Veneto and sipped my way around the Spanish stairs, finally narrowing my selection down to twenty cafés, then to two.

Caffé Greco is a 200-year-old bastion of red velvet, refinement and fine manners where the dour waiters wear tails, and open their wallets to give you change with the same action of a priest opening a prayer book. If you sit still long enough, some starving artist will probably draw you, to add to the framed etchings, poems and paintings on the walls.

The coffee is very good, and comes in fine china on a tray, always with an accompanying glass of water.

A much, much, much cheaper, and marginally better coffee comes from the busy machines at the *torrefazione* (coffee-roasting house) Tazza d'Oro, Natalia Fiocchetto's most Roman of Roman cafés near the Pantheon.

It's hard to explain, but an espresso coffee tastes so much better when you're standing at an elbow-height bar, wedged between a nun on one side and three extravagantly uniformed *caribinieri* (police) on the other. That's when I knew I belonged to this country, deep down, somewhere near the small intestine, and that this was my true family. But if you're not Italian, I don't expect you to understand.

"Without fat, we wouldn't have potato chips, cashew nuts, crème brûlée, rillettes, terrines, fried chicken, Yorkshire pud. Or Marlon Brando or Dawn French, for that matter."

Fat-finding tour

For me, Ms Right is, in fact, Mrs Sprat. If only we had met earlier, we could now be sizzling our marbled steaks and tossing our peas in butter until the cows came home. Then we could milk the cows and churn cream together to have with our morning pancakes.

Sadly she is already taken, by a moron called Jack, who could eat no fat. I know the type well. The sort who orders Caesar salad with the dressing on the side; who cuts those cute juicy little tails off lamb chops, and who insists on having the skin taken off the chicken, when all sensible people would prefer to have the chicken taken off the skin.

But we need fat. We run on fat. Fat is an essential part of a balanced diet, providing essential fatty acids and important fat-soluble vitamins such as A, D, E and K. Some fatty acids convert into molecules known as phospholipids (the basic material of cell membranes) which are essential for the proper functioning of our brain cells.

Blah, blah, blah. Forget all that. What's important is that without fat, we wouldn't have potato chips, cashew nuts, crème brûlée, rillettes, terrines, fried chicken, Yorkshire pud. Or Marlon Brando or Dawn French, for that matter.

Intent on making fat the next enemy, the fatophobic are fast turning it into the next drug of choice. When fat is no longer legally available, it goes underground. It turns up in bread, toasted muesli and chocolate biscuits. It mutates into seemingly innocuous additives that may not be as innocent as they seem.

I prefer fat I can see. That way, I can cut it off if there is too much, or leave it to protect the meat as it cooks. I can choose the quality of my fat, in the same way as I choose the quality of my fruit, vegetables and wine. I can also judge my intake of fat, so that every now and then, I can indulge in Fat's Finest Moments, without ending up in the cholesterol corner of Casualty.

Look at confit, for instance. Originally a sensible, housewifely way of preserving duck or goose over the lean (sorry) months of winter, confit has a miraculous by-product—flavour. After salting the meat and gently simmering it in its own rendered fat, it tastes juicy, bright, and strong. Without confit, cassoulet is a bean stew.

The Italians use fat to preserve and prolong their enjoyment of pork. They squeeze it into the spicy salami of the south, the elegant cotechino sausages of the north, and those delicate logs of mortadella from Bologna. The height of fat chic is to eat cubes of polenta at Verona's Antica Bottega del Vino, each one draped with a butterfly-thin layer of cured fat that clings like damp gossamer to the golden sides as it melts over the charcoal grill.

So much of great cooking is merely the dissembling and transformation of fat. What Pierre Koffmann has done with the pig's foot goes way beyond the bar-room expectations of Bessie Smith. Stuffed with sweetbreads, chicken farce and morels, each delicate trotter wallows in a lipsticky sauce that is three-star fat on a plate.

There is even time in China, between eating dishes of lightly cooked vegetables and steamed fish, to create ways of cooking fat that amaze and delight. Take Dong Po pork, from the mystical West Lake city of Hangzhou. Named after the Sung Dynasty reformer and poet Su Dong Po (or Su Tung Po), this is fatty belly pork cooked for four hours with shaohsing rice wine, ginger, sugar and soy sauce until it is wobbily, shimmeringly translucent. Eating it, you can't help but feel that you are restoring to your body what life, the universe, the traffic and doing your tax returns have taken out. It is truly restorative.

Su's 'In Praise of Pork' is the most poetic recipe ever written about fat:

Firewood smouldering, the fire dimly gleams
Hurry it not, let it slowly simmer
When cooked long enough it will be beautiful.

There is only one poem more moving, but if you don't mind, it is one I would rather not discuss. It still hurts too much.

"Many attempt this journey and fail. Many more don't even realise it is a journey. But I have now Arrived. I refer, of course, to my current and, I suspect, my last, toaster-in-residence."

■ The dark side

It's a bit like a boy and his dog. There is a bond that exists between a man and his toaster that is thicker than blood; a bond that goes way beyond mere convenience. It is a bond that comes simply from knowing that each will be there for the other, no matter what.

Yes, I am one of the toaster-dependent. It is, after all, one of the few pieces of machinery that I can operate. It has seen me through thick and thin, through rye and sourdough, through bagel and crumpet.

In spite of witnessing me at my worst (early in the morning and late at night) it never ceases to be bright, gleaming and truly efficient. After all, a toaster can turn something uncooked into something cooked in around ninety seconds—that's faster than a microwave. It's a miracle. Better still, it's a miracle spread with butter.

My toaster may have changed its physical form over the years, but my relationship with it hasn't altered. It has survived the swing-door stage, the pop-up era, the retro chic second-hand job, even the ironic postmodern reproduction.

The best of them all was an ancient, skinny, flip-door manual toaster. My bread used to love it. Because there was air around the slice as it cooked, it never got all steamy, which seems to happen in the new high-tech machines.

Sadly, it had one minor fault. If you took your eye off it even for a second to glance at the newspaper headlines, or to add milk to your coffee, it would notify you that your toast was cooked by sending out great billowing waves of acrid smoke.

In the meantime, I have flirted with toaster ovens, and burnt my fingers on toast and sandwich makers. I have grilled bread on and under grillers, attached it to hand-twisted wire forks over campfires, and attempted to toast a crumpet on a gas flame during a power strike.

While I didn't realise it at the time, I was going through a very necessary journey, treading a crumb-strewn path towards the pinnacle of achievement: the perfect, the ultimate toaster. Many attempt this journey and fail. Many more don't even realise it is a journey. But I have now Arrived. I refer, of course, to my current, and I suspect my last, toaster-in-residence. The Dualit.

Only the country that built the Morris Minor, the Spitfire and the Rolls Royce engine could have produced the Dualit. This is where good bread wants to go when it dies. This is toaster nirvana.

Invented in 1946 (it takes a good war to produce a good toaster) by engineer Max Gort-Barten in his London workshop, it is a twentieth-century classic that is destined to toast well into the twenty-first. It is virtually unchanged from the refinements made to the original modelling in the 1950s, and every handmade unit is stamped with the assembler's individual mark.

What I like most about it, apart from the fact that it looks like an armoured car with slots in the top, is that there are no dark or light control knobs, no fancy extras, and no pop-up mechanisms that scare the life out of you if you have just the tiniest hangover.

Instead, it employs a timer and a 'stay-warm mechanical ejector', which is Dualit-speak for a lever. It means that after the timer has turned off the high temperature panels with etched foil heating circuits, the toast stays warm inside the toaster until you have finished reading the headlines, or stirring milk into your tea. There is a crumb tray that slides out for easy cleaning, and an adjustable foot for uneven kitchen surfaces (handy if you haven't cleaned up the crumbs for a month or two).

I had to sell the car in order to pay for it, but that is neither here nor there. With the price of bread these days, you can't be too careful.

"I picked up the eye with my chopsticks and placed it in my mouth. After about a hundred years, I swallowed, and discovered that it did indeed taste like an oyster."

■ The best bit

'House special!' announced the Japanese restaurateur with pride, bearing a giant ceramic bowl in which lay half a giant fish head awash in light soupy juices. It was as if I had never tasted fish before. It tasted not only of the sea, but as if it were still in it; delicate yet forceful, single-minded yet complex. My chopsticks thrashed around the bowl like piranha, careful to strip off the rich, gelatinous cheek, and the juicy flesh around the severed neck.

The owner was horrified. Instead of taking away what was left in the bowl, he stared down at it in utter bewilderment.

'But you've left the best bit,' he said. Best bit? All that was left was a little connective tissue, a few bones and one rather large eye. I entered my own private suspense movie. Cut from my appalled expression to MCU fish eye. Cut back to my face, but closer, then back to ECU fish eye; in which you could see the reflection of my appalled expression.

'Tastes just like oyster, only better,' said the restaurateur. I picked up the eye in my chopsticks and placed it in my mouth. After about a hundred years, I swallowed, and discovered that it did indeed taste like an oyster. I never left the best bit again.

But how many best bits had I unknowingly left behind out of unwillingness or ignorance, until then?

I made a fool of myself over my very first Shanghai hairy crab in Hong Kong one winter. Having picked out the sweet, succulent, ginger-fragrant flesh, I put down my chopsticks. My host blushed for me, before pointing to the roe-laden head shell, explaining that it was the eggs that made the crab such a delicacy.

'Tastes just like scrambled eggs, only better,' he said. And of course, he was right. He then pointed to my discarded prawn heads from a delightful dish of prawns steamed in their shells.

'But you've left the best bit,' he said as he picked up one of the heads and sucked like a vacuum cleaner.

The trouble is, one culture's best bits is another culture's garbage. In Spain, pigs' ears are cooked in a delicious, addictive casserole with pigs' trotters and chorizo sausages. In other countries, you can't even buy a pig's ear, much less turn it into such a silk purse of a dish.

In Beijing, duck feet are boned and tossed in a salad with cucumbers and yellow mustard sauce, while in Guangzhou, steamed and braised chicken feet are the juiciest stars of the dim sum trolleys. In a Greek home, one is honoured to be served the head of the spit-roasted lamb, especially if it comes complete with tongue and brains. Nor would a Greek home throw out the stems and leaves of the beetroot, but simply treat them as a beautiful vegetable that requires a little steaming and a dressing of olive oil and lemon juice while still warm.

There are some best bits we are all very well aware of, like the curl of orange coral on a sea scallop, the fatty tail of a grill-scorched lamb chop, and the luscious bone marrow in osso buco. I always try the rind of a white mould cheese such as gratte-paille or brie de Meaux. If not ammoniacal, it gives me the wonderfully peculiar feeling of biting into cumulus clouds.

Even inedible rinds, such as the boot leather rind of a Parmigiano Reggiano is never wasted in Italy, but cleaned up and tossed into the makings of a minestrone soup, where it softens over the long cooking and leaves its ineffably fine flavour.

Determined never to leave the best bit, I now curiously eye off any old fish tail, potato peelings or leftover egg shells, just in case I'm missing out. My finest moment came at the end of a dish of deer penis, an entire platter of something that I'm sure even the deer would consider their best bits. Left on the plate was a perfect little sea horse, about the length of my little finger.

'You left the best bit,' I said to my fellow diners, as I popped it in my mouth and crunched. They looked aghast.

'That was the garnish,' they cried. 'Ah,' I said, recovering immediately, 'tastes just like decoration, only better.'

"If you're not sure what constitutes the ignoble art of nerdy food, then picture yourself eating it in public. If you can't, it's nerdy. Nerdy food is a private pleasure, best practised with blinds drawn."

◼ Cuisine du nerd

O ne cannot live exclusively on a diet of baked leek and *trompette* tart, roast turbot marinated in spicy lime and coconut, cabbage-wrapped pork knuckle with sauce *gribiche*, *velouté* of artichokes with foie gras, roast wood pigeon with the perfume of cèpes, and pineapple *millefeuille* with coconut sorbet.

It's not good for you. The average human body can only take so much fashionable food before the various systems start shutting down. Sooner or later, the fine food receptors get frayed and thin, and the jus diviners lose their intensity. The nasal fragrance detectors start breaking down; and the cappuccino sauce selective channel gets stretched and flabby from over-use.

That's where nerdy food comes in. We need nerdy food to counteract the toxins and to reinstate the brain cell loss caused by an excessive intake of modish food and wine. The idea goes right back to that ancient see-saw of Chinese culture, the *yin* and *yang* thing. The Chinese believe that food, as with all things in life, should be a balance between the *yin* and the *yang*, the twin forces that ultimately control our lives. *Yin* is the feminine force. It is cooling, comforting and dark. *Yang* is masculine, symbolised by heat, light and energy. That makes fashionable food very *yang*ish, with its adrenalin-rush service and look-at-me presentation, leaving all that hard *yin* work to be done by nerdy food.

So a fricassée of lobster with potato gratin needs to be offset as soon as possible by something like split pea and ham soup, or maybe some smoked oysters straight from the tin. A risotto of nettles with asparagus spears and black truffles can be countered rather nicely by a good old-fashioned kedgeree, pink with tomato ketchup.

A northern banquet of drunken chicken, Peking Duck and squirrel-cut fish will reach your *yang*y parts, but only fried rice will get to the parts banquet cuisine cannot reach. Likewise, *boudin noir* with Puy lentils requires curried sausages. Bouillabaisse needs to be offset by a bowl of mulligatawny. Anything with foie gras can easily be countered by anything with HP sauce. You get the picture.

Don't tell me you don't achieve a balance in every other area of your life. You may step out in your Paul Smiths and your Patrick Coxes to see the latest Polish arthouse film on Monday night, but by Wednesday night you're staying in, curled up in the cooking-stained tracksuit and your dog-chewed trainers watching *The Bill*.

If you're not sure what constitutes the ignoble art of nerdy food, then picture yourself eating it in public. If you can't, it's nerdy. Nerdy food is a private pleasure, best practised with the blinds drawn and the telephone off the hook.

The worst thing to happen to nerdy food is that—ye gods—it is now fashionable. England's Nigel Bloody Slater started it, with all his spoon-licking and sticky puddings. Simon Bloody Hopkinson did a whole book on it. Jamie Oliver did a fry-up on prime-time television, for heaven's sake. Now everybody's doing it. They think it's chic, in a we-know-what-we're-doing-is-ironic way.

But do they realise what they are doing? Do they not understand the tide of history, the great cycle of humanity? If they force nerdy food out of the kitchen closet and onto the television screens and into the designer dining rooms of the gastroscenti, then *yin* can't do its thing with *yang* and the whole country is up the spout. The natural order of things is all but scuttled.

And we all know what would happen then. There we would be, in our baggy tracksuit pants in the latest cutting-edge downtown restaurant, scoffing down heat 'n' serve pizza. With cups of tea.

That leaves the noisettes of lamb with provençale herbs and a red wine glaze for Sunday-night tea at home, with the two of you dressed in Collette Dinnigan and Helmut Lang, listening to Wynton Marsalis. Which is probably how the world should be, when you come to think of it.

"Order something you've never had before. Better still, order something you've never heard of before. Convention is there to be flouted. Convention loves to be flouted."

Lights, camera, dinner

You know that bit in restaurant reviews when they talk about the scene, the buzz, the vibe, the atmosphere? Well, that's us.

We're a part of that peculiar, all-important chemistry that can miraculously convert dinner into dining. Our role in that chemistry is as important as that of the chef, the waiters, the music and the décor.

Like it or not, the role of being a diner brings with it certain obligations. People who go to a restaurant expecting to be amused, entertained or otherwise distracted just don't get it. Ah, but people who go expecting to be amusing, entertaining or otherwise distracting are well on the way to fulfilling the obligations of a diner.

Caffé Greco in Rome's Via Condotti has been attracting a fascinating cast of patrons, inevitably described as Fellini-esque, for most of its 240 years. You may recall it is where I sought my long-lost Italian relatives, who would definitely have been Fellini-esque. Go on a good day, and there will be velvet-suited children politely nibbling sandwiches under the friezes and framed poems in the gilt-edged parlours, as bow-tied waiters carry trays of silver pots to ancient dowagers.

Go on a bad day, and you will be surrounded by a huge crowd of tourists who want to get in on the action and be a part of the scene, if only for a moment. It's social graffiti of the worst kind. They turn up in their lurid yellow plastic weatherproof jackets, slump their back-pack deformities onto the marble floor, order a breathtakingly expensive coke and sit back waiting for the show to begin. Well, of course, they are disappointed. They *are* the show. They may as well have stayed home.

The same thing happens when a new restaurant suddenly gets a reputation for star-spotting. When Keith McNally's faux-Parisian Balthazar bistro opened in New York, it instantly became a hangout for Jerry Seinfeld and a supporting cast of minor celebs.

By the time I got there, three months later, the place was filled to the breadboards with lifeless extras who became animated on cue only when the door was opened. Nope, not Jerry. They sank back into lethargy when it was only me, or another one of them.

Look at the interiors of the latest batch of new restaurants. They're fun, quirky, eccentric and attention-grabbing. Why? Because the designers know that without television, we need something to look at.

By just sitting there, we rob the places of their energy,

life and character. We take all, give nothing. Keep taking without giving anything back, and pretty soon, there's not going to be much left. No wonder they need lots of décor.

Dining out is theatre, drama, showbiz, performance art. Like a night at the theatre, it can be engaging, stimulating and provocative, or it can be sleep-inducing, tedious and wearisome. If you're not looking forward to it, then please, stay home.

One of the reasons I return to my local café is because there is a woman at the café right next door I adore looking at. She has jet black hair, often in a braid, a joyously Roman nose, and always, always, always, bright scarlet lips. If she turned up without the lips, she would only be a nose. The lips are her contribution to the almost painterly tableau she creates by sitting against a stained old wall of framed photographs with her espresso coffee. My café experience would be less without her. I can only hope that I am as interesting a part of the décor for her.

Sometimes it's hard. You just want to hide, you're feeling low, you're having an off night, you gave at the office. All the more reason to allow the special dynamics of a restaurant to save you from yourself. Order something you've never had before. Better still, order something you've never heard of before. Champagne helps, but by all means, drink what you like. Convention is there to be flouted. Convention loves to be flouted. Don't stare at that fascinating table over there. Be that fascinating table. Dining out is not a spectator sport. Everyone can play.

"It was so rich, he named it for the richest man he knew. I wonder, however, if Mr Rockefeller was all that thrilled about being transformed into a snail substitute."

Something to remember me by

Is it asking too much that long after I am gone, my name will be remembered with fondness and affection? That it will somehow play a part in the lives of people I will never meet? Of course not.

Immortality is pretty tricky stuff. Wanting it is one thing, but getting it is another matter altogether. There are no more countries left to discover, all the peaks have been climbed, and really, a round-the-world solo sailor is more of a nuisance than a heroic figure these days.

The traditional method is to do something miraculously wonderful and worthwhile that will change the world forever. I tried to do that last Thursday and nobody noticed, so I guess that one's out.

There is only one surefire way. I have to get some fabulous, high-profile celebrity chef to create a dish and name it in my honour. Maybe Tetsuya, Charlie or Gordon could whip up something after service one night.

It's a pity Auguste Escoffier isn't still around, or he could have done for me what he did for the Australian opera singer, Dame Nellie Melba, in 1892.

When the Duke of Orleans held a special dinner at the Savoy Hotel to honour Melba's performance in Wagner's *Lohengrin*, the great chef pulled out all the stops. Inspired by the singer's greatness, and the potential for publicity, Escoffier created a gloriously kitsch vision of a carved ice swan floating on a sea of vanilla ice-cream, bearing plump, ripe, poached peaches draped in raspberry coulis. Topping it off was a fine, silky web of spun sugar. The original recipe has evolved into canned peach slices on commercial ice-cream with raspberry syrup, but the thing is, her name is still on the menu, over one hundred years later.

Then there are people like the American millionaire, John D. Rockefeller, who could have bought and sold his immortality a hundred times over. Yet when we remember his name today, we think not of oil wells, railroads or steel plants, but of a lush, classy dish of warmed oysters enrobed in a puréed sauce of green herbs and vegetables.

Jules Alciatore of Antoine's restaurant in New Orleans created Oysters Rockefeller in 1899 when he was threatened by a shortage of snails from France for his famous *escargots bourguignon*. It was so rich, he named it for the richest man he knew. I wonder, however, if Mr Rockefeller was all that thrilled about being commemorated as a snail substitute.

Far better to be remembered as a man of substance and extravagance like Gioachino Rossini. While opera lovers may remember every note of the *Barber of Seville*, my thoughts go to the Parisian chef who, in 1855, responded to Rossini's request for 'something with foie gras and truffles' by creating the timeless tournedos Rossini.

Some restaurants, like the great Harry's Bar in Venice, make a habit of immortalising people. Although the restaurant's famous dish of thin raw slices of beef with a light creamy sauce owes its origins to an ailing countess whose doctor had forbidden her to eat cooked meat, it owes its name to an artist famed for his vivid use of red and white: Vittore Carpaccio.

Since the 1930s, the most popular summer drink at Harry's was a deliciously rosy concoction of sparkling Prosecco wine and white peach juice. It remained nameless until an exhibition opened in 1948 honouring a painter known for his rich, poetic colours. His name, (Giovanni) Bellini, is now on everyone's lips, every summer, around the world.

I don't care what my namesake is, as long as it looks good, tastes good and has real staying power. Something that really sums up my character: large yet graceful; complex yet simple. I would prefer something chocolate, so that I can be remembered as tall, dark and slightly bitter, but unkind people have suggested an entire buffet would be more appropriate.

"Another friend used to make the ultimate cauliflower cheese by steaming an entire cauliflower, then pouring the thickest, cheesiest sauce over it, and devouring the lot in bed. Well, it was me, actually."

Dinner
for one

'You won't be back for another two days? No, don't worry about me, I'm fine. I've got a bit of work I should do. What? Oh, there's probably something in the fridge to eat.'

Is there a poorer, more pathetic creature than your average suddenly-turned-single? This is one of nature's lost and lonely souls, someone to be pitied and prayed for, someone unloved, unwanted and unaccompanied; the very essence of unmitigated misery and abandon.

Are you kidding?

Lurking just below this wretched exterior is another being who is deliriously happy. After all, there is no-one to say with the lift of an eyebrow that you can't watch the *X-Files*. No-one with whom you have to make polite idle chatter. No-one with whom you have to remember to say things like 'with whom'. And absolutely no-one to say that they do not feel like crumbed brains and crisp bacon for dinner.

You can do what you want. You can whip your clothes off and leave them on the floor, turn up the music, and eat and drink anything you like.

The only problem is that the pressure of all this freedom can be quite devastating. Inevitably, you go completely overboard on the first evening.

One friend used to make enough chocolate mousse for a dinner party for six, then eat the whole thing with a large spoon. Another friend used to make the ultimate cauliflower cheese by steaming an entire cauliflower then pouring the thickest, cheesiest sauce over it, and devouring the lot in bed. Well, it was me, actually. So was the other friend.

American writer Nora Ephron captured the scene agonisingly accurately in her book and film *Heartburn*, in which the heroine Rachel Samstat (Meryl Streep) is home alone, while her womanising husband (Jack Nicholson) is out on the town. There she sits, with a saucepan of extremely buttery mashed potato in her lap, which she eats while crying her eyes out watching a weepie video.

My wife can relate, if only to the food aspect. If I ever leave her alone for an evening, I am replaced by a baking tray of garlicky, rosemary-scented roasted vegetables — sweet potato, pumpkin, onions, potatoes and loads of parsnip — that are then artfully arranged in a pyramid on a plate, with sprigs of fresh rosemary added at the last minute. With it, she drinks Campari and soda. Don't go looking for flavour matches or anything logical. These are not the nights to be logical. The point is that it makes her feel less alone. In fact, she loves it so much, she keeps asking me when I'm going away.

It's not quite so simple for some of us. I find I run to three basic stages. The first stage is the first night, when I'm revelling in the fact that I don't actually have to do anything stupid like drink from a glass. All I have do is throw some rice and water in my trusty Chinese rice cooker and wait for it to smell good, then bung in some sliced *lup cheong* sausage and a finely chopped spring onion and leave them alone for ten minutes. Put some soy on the side, and a Tsing Tao beer or ten, and dinner is served.

By the second night, I'm ready to develop the sausage theme further. There is something about your humble breakfast snag that few women understand, so they tend to taste better when you're on your own. This gets the gravy treatment, the mountain of mash and the Cascade Pale Ale. At least some of us think of flavour matching.

If it's been a few days and there's not much sport on the telly, I progress to the third stage, and actually cook something. Such as *vincisgrassi*, a rich sort of lasagne full of things like sheeps' brains and sweetbreads, and other stuff that generally warrant another lift of the eyebrow when I suggest them for dinner.

I'll even put out a tablecloth and sip fine Burgundy, from a glass and everything. It's usually about that time that she rings, from wherever.

'No, don't worry about me, I'm fine. I've got a bit of work I should do. What? Oh, there's probably something in the fridge to eat.'

"There are only so many foods that you can stuff down your gob and still be held a respectable, accountable human being. Chips, yes. Seared duck breast with cherries, no."

Chips in the night

N ever eat out with your psychologist. It seems they don't have to rely on those Rorschach inkblot tests any more to find out all about your innermost feelings. All they have to do is take you out to dinner.

According to a recent newspaper interview with a London psychologist, your food cravings tell the trained eye as much about your emotional hunger as your physical hunger.

So you thought you wanted that big slice of chocolate cake because you needed a sugar hit? No. The truth, according to the anonymous psychologist, is that you are feeling insecure, and quite possibly experiencing some serious relationship problems.

Craving pizza with double anchovies means you have financial problems. Jam doughnuts signify stress. Tea with sugar means you're not getting the recognition you deserve. Creamy salad dressing? You're suffering depression, exasperation, frustration. Lasagne? A desire to shield yourself. And a craving for baked beans, apparently, signifies a desire for a holiday or change of career.

Sadly, the article didn't mention one of the western world's strongest cravings—for the humble hot potato chip—but it can't be too hard to work that one out for ourselves.

Hot potato chips are the ultimate pacifier. We all crave their crusty/softness, their salty tang, their self-indulgent, play-time, kids' party associations. Put a bowl of them in front of a group of noisy, chatty people, and a smug, fat silence will fall almost immediately, but for the soft little hoo and ha you can hear as people blow on them to cool them before stuffing them down their gobs.

Because that's the thing about chips. There are only so many foods that you can stuff down your gob and still be held a respectable, accountable human being. Peanuts, yes. Jelly beans, yes. Sandwiches, yes. Seared duck breast with cherries, no.

Let us now define chips, for the purposes of gob-stuffing. Fat, chunky potato wedges are not chips. Anything dusted in Cajun spices and served with sour cream is not a chip. Waffle-cut wafers are not chips, nor are those tricksy potato nests. Nor do I include fat-free, oven-baked, no mess, no fuss, frozen packet chip wannabes.

Your honest-to-goodness chip should be cut by hand from a good old Sebago, Russet Burbank or King Edward potato, washed to rid it of its starch, dried thoroughly and cooked once, in good, fresh oil to cook the potato, and again, to crisp the chip.

There is only one way to cook chips successfully at home, and that is to invest in a full-scale commercial chip fryer with a built-in temperature gauge. Next, you will need a constant supply of ten-litre drums of first-rate vegetable or peanut oil on hand.

In other words, go out for your chips. Your average domestic chip-fryer holds too little oil to maintain a high enough temperature throughout the cooking. The oil is a nuisance, the smell even more so, and the cleaning up a bore. The chips themselves are only great for about twenty seconds before they go soft.

Restaurant chips, on the other hand, last the whole meal through, softening only towards the end of your steak, burger, fish or chicken. The French like to eat their *pommes frites* towards the end of the meal, smashing them into the leftover sauce and eating them neatly with knife and fork. Problems only arise if they are dining with Brits or Americans, in which case there are none left by the end of the meal. It's a chromosome thing. We non-French tend to eat them as extra-curricular treats, our hands sneaking out automatically for more in the same way we turn to our glasses for a sip of wine.

Making great *pommes frites* is the natural birthright of most French bistro chefs. My best were in Lyons, at a bistro near the station called La Mere Vittet. Then there was a chip epiphany on the streets of Amsterdam, when I bought a paper cone of chips from a street vendor and watched, horrified, as he tossed a slug of mayonnaise over the lot. I was back for more in twenty minutes.

There were the tiny thin matchstick chips tossed with deep-fried baby prawns at Saltwater restaurant, a sundrenched bistro at Noosa on the Sunshine Coast. And the inevitable *moules et frites* in a Belgian café, from those funny people who insist they invented French fries.

Clearly, a deep craving for a basket of crisp, golden chips says only one thing about you: that you are perfectly normal.

The apple
of my eye

Well, *of course*, an apple a day would keep the
doctor away. Why would a member of the medical profession, renowned for its gastronomic
tendencies, make a house call for a mere apple?

Ah, but slice that dreary apple into thin slivers,
arrange it on a disc of puff pastry, scatter with sugar,
brush with melted butter, and bake it. By the time the
pastry is crisp and flaky, the edges are golden and the
apple is velvety, caramelised and a little scorched, you'll
be getting medicos on your doorstep until way past mid-
night. The very physician to whom you were merely
4 p.m. in a leather-bound appointment diary will suddenly be tucking his cashmere car rug about your knees,
and asking after your mother.

Mind you, if I were an apple, I'd want to be a tart. An
apple without pastry is a Schumacher without a Ferrari.
He may be a good walker, but it's not the point. A fine,

"A fine, crisp tart is the only fitting culmination of a life lived to the core. It's the greatest height an apple can reach once it has fallen from the tree of knowledge."

crisp tart — *tarte fine aux pommes* — is the only fitting culmination of a life lived to the core. It is the greatest height an apple can reach once it has fallen from the tree of knowledge.

Not being an apple, I console myself by eating as many apple tarts as humanly possible. On one fourteen-day driving trip through France, I personally accounted for the destruction of eighteen of the country's finest. Based on an average cooking time of *vingt* minutes per tart, my companion claimed that I had robbed her of six hours good shopping time. I retaliated by saying that the choosing and ordering of an apple tart is good shopping time in itself, but apparently it doesn't measure up to fingering through the little cashmere thingies at agnès b.

Because an apple tart is composed of so few ingredients, each one must be perfect: the apple sufficiently acidic, and the pastry thin, with that faint backbite of salt. The heat must be sufficient to allow the butter from the pastry to ooze out and mingle with the released apple juices and sugar, the whole caramelising into one glorious toffeed, winey, appley bite.

Other tarts come close to such divinity. The 'upside-down' tarte Tatin is an ingenious creation from the resourceful Tatin sisters, who in the early twentieth century ran a hotel restaurant in the small French town of Lamotte-Beuvron in Sologne. Apparently the kitchen didn't run to a baking oven, so the sisters hit on the idea of cooking the apples in a pan on top of the stove. Pastry beneath the apple would have burnt, but pastry on top, they discovered, could be cooked under a metal dome. The molten, lava-like goo of apples under the crisp pastry hat is heavenly, and one could live for three days on the fragrant steam alone, but I can't help thinking it might have been easier to buy an oven and make it properly.

Lionel Pôilane's rustic little apple tartlettes in Paris, the creamy apple and custard tarts of Normandy, and the pastry-encased whole apples from Anjou known as *bourdaines* all stretch our idea of what constitutes a tart, but we accept such discrepancies with pleasure.

As for the Viennese *apfelstrudel*, the concept may be Hungarian and the parchment-thin pastry may be Turkish in origin, but it's still a very nice tart — with fried breadcrumbs, sugar, sultanas and cinnamon — rolled up.

The tart — originally from *tourte* — is undeniably French, although ye olde apple pie has been traced to Elizabethan times in England, which makes 'as American as apple pie' sound a bit like 'as Ukrainian as pavlova'.

Whatever form it may take, and whatever name it may acquire, the combination of apple and pastry proves to be one of the most alluring humanity has yet engineered. Throw in a glass of Sauternes, and we may well revolutionise the medical care system yet.

pleasure
& satisfaction

"Only a picnic will restore us. We need to wiggle our toes in warm golden sand or tickly green grass, to lie on our backs and dream the world back into the sort of place it used to be."

■ Back to nature

We need picnics. We need, just for a few hours, to feel free, natural, primitive and unencumbered. We need to leave manners and etiquette and protocol and red tape behind us, and go bare-footed, hungry and sticky into the wilderness.

By the end of a hard week, it is human nature to want to shed ourselves of all our worldly urban trappings, to disentangle ourselves from the endless bits and pieces of hardware and software that surround us. We need to breathe fresh air instead of carbon monoxide and after-shave and oven spray, and get away from the beeps, trills and screams of mobile phones, pagers, Walkmans and computer games.

We need to wiggle our toes in warm golden sand or tickly green grass, to lie on our backs and dream the world back into the sort of place it used to be.

If we have a particularly severe case of end-of-week-itis, only a picnic will restore us. All those primal urges can be satisfied: to feel fire at our fingertips; gather twigs; drink water from a stream instead of a tap. To run and skip and jump in the air, and to nod off under a kindly tree when we get tired. We don't want to do it forever. Ooh, no. Half a day is more than enough for sliding down grassy paths; pushing aside bracken and just sitting on top of a hill with not another person in sight. Except, perhaps, another person sitting on top of another faraway hill, like the Little Prince in Antoine de Saint Exupery's famously adult children's story.

Now, how do we go about it? First, the food. It should be plain and simple and honest, something you can clutch in one hand while you shade your eyes against the sun with the other. A good old-fashioned ham sandwich on white bread would be perfect. And a perfectly ripe red tomato, for that little extra sting of summer, with a few flakes of sea salt to draw out its juices. Perhaps a leaf or two of basil? No, better would be an easily portable jar of pesto. We could whip that up quickly before we go.

But it's not a picnic without a fat wedge of egg and bacon pie, the centre still warm and soft, and the bacon smoky and salty. If you blind-bake the pastry the night before, you could finish it off just before you leave. And you might as well do an old-fashioned veal and ham pie while you're at it, which reminds me, you had better pack a sharp knife, and some mustard, and maybe some pickles.

Mmm, mustard. What about a big piece of rare roast beef, crusted with crushed peppercorns? Very hunter-gatherer, extremely primal. And potato salad on the side, made with whole egg mayo and snipped green chives? Not so primal, but very nice.

And a bottle of good white, nothing too fancy—there is nobody you have to impress sitting on top of a hill, your toes wiggling in the grass—a friendly little sauv blanc, perhaps. Something citrussy, green and herbaceous. Mind you, that means you should take some cheese, maybe a hunk of Gruyère or Parmigiano or some cloth-bound cheddar. That could lead on to some fresh fruit, perhaps a perfect peach. And a few amaretti biscuits to have with coffee. Perhaps a dessert wine?

Then there are a few other little essentials you'll need to take. The tartan picnic blanket, of course. And what if the tickly grass is damp, or full of burrs, or sheep droppings? Maybe the fold-away chairs and table would be handy. Mosquito repellent? Check. Those little wipey things? Check. Flask for tea? Check. Milk and sugar, check. Butter, or extra-virgin olive oil if it's too warm for the butter. Lemons, just because. A few plates, good wine glasses (even sauv blanc tends to go funny in anodised aluminium), a corkscrew, a book or two, a hat, and something warm in case the weather turns, check.

Finally, the moment comes. The car is filled to the roof with half the contents of your garage and laundry. The kitchen has been transferred to the boot. It's just three stops at various places on the way out of town for ice, maps and a gas refill for the portable stove, and you're on your way.

Free at last.

"Who on earth came up with the term plain flour? I've never seen anything more complicated. It is a world of lipids and glutens; a world that belongs to laboratories and research grants."

Fear of flouring

There I was, a fully grown (and then some) adult who knew his way around the trusty four-burner and the old fan-forced convection oven as if born to the task. I was a walking, talking, cooking machine. The fiddlier and trickier the recipe, the better I could do it. If you wanted a genuine tripes *à la mode de Caen*, simmered long and lovingly all day in its cidery juices, I was your man. A corn-fed chicken prepared 'in half mourning' (with truffles pushed under the breast), and cooked *en vessie* in a pig's bladder? Not a problem.

Before you could say eight-jewelled duck, the duck would be tunnel-boned, the glutinous rice juicily steamed, and the whole thing stuffed, sewn up, braised, served and carved.

But ask for a cake, brioche, tart or pie, and I would turn to jelly.

It's a flour thing. Whenever I went near the stuff, I could feel my confidence sag, my self-esteem evaporate and my sense of usefulness shrivel to nothing. It was kryptonite to my superman. It was my undipped Achilles heel. It was my *bête blanc*.

I took consolation in the fact that flour is about chemistry, and not cooking. It is a world of lipids and glutens; a world that belongs to professors, laboratories, and expensive research grants. Who on earth came up with the term 'plain flour'? I've never seen anything more complicated.

God knows, I tried to defeat my fear of flouring. I could overcome the terror long enough to do a decent white sauce, or thicken a gravy, but when the task resembled anything remotely connected to a dough, I ran a mile.

Even the most hardened trade unionist would not set down the kind of working conditions demanded by dough. For one, it refuses to work if it gets too hot.

Next, there's the workplace. No nice little timber workbench or plastic cutting boards for flour, oh no. Only an expensive investment in marble or granite will help it keep its cool.

After it finally does a bit of work, it suddenly demands a thirty-minute rest break. Try pushing it around, and it breaks down, losing its elasticity.

So I did the only thing possible: moved to a nicer neighbourhood with a pâtisserie at the end of the street.

And then it happened. One Christmas, someone who knew nothing about my affliction gave me one of those little pasta makers with the dinky little clamp that you attach to the kitchen bench. Terrifying, but very cute. By Boxing Day I had the thing set up. By Easter, I got around to using it.

Dutifully, I made a well in the flour and broke in the eggs, cautiously dipping my immaculately clean fingertips into the whole she-bang, expecting it to feel icky and yucky. Instead, it actually felt rather nice, all soft and talcum powdery. So I started wriggling and pushing and prodding and rubbing. Before my eyes, floury became crumbly, crumbly became clumpy, and clumpy became an unholy mess that seemed to stretch from kitchen to second bedroom.

I felt like a four-year-old who had failed play-dough. Waaaah! I don't want to play any more! I threw a little tantrum, smashing my clenched fists into the dough and sending it crashing onto the table. Never again, never again, beat the rhythm of my flailing hands, until . . . hmmmm. I suddenly noticed the dough had achieved a sudden sheen, a glossy smoothness. It was beautiful! It was round! It was dough!

After a well-earned rest for both of us, I proceeded to make perfect pasta. Thank you, lipids and glutens, whoever you are.

From there, things were pretty much a cake walk. First came scones (a mild hissy fit was all it took), then Italian biscotti (fairly serious domestic dispute with my wife), then, one wonderful day, brioche (utter fury at the local council). Now I can do anything, as long as I can throw a complete wobbly. And they say that working with dough is relaxing.

"There is no trick to matching food and wine. It is not unlike other forms of matchmaking. Don't, whatever you do, consult an expert. They are completely confused by the matter."

■ Striking matches

I n a life that has embraced more dinner parties than most people have hot dinners, I have been lucky enough to encounter some of the great minds of our time, whose knives and forks have been set next to mine. I have dined with artists whose merest flick of paint on a canvas would fetch a hundred thousand at Sotheby's. I have discussed politics with heads of state, the future of the novel with writers who have done much to destroy it, and the ethics of uranium mining with a nuclear physicist.

Yet these people — geniuses in their own fields, capable of splitting either atoms or infinitives before breakfast — were dodos when it came to the table. They had absolutely no idea of what wine to drink with the food they were eating.

Some just drank what was put in front of them, while others stuck to the 'I like Bordeaux so I'm going to drink it with everything' approach. One had given up alto-gether and drank Sprite throughout the meal.

But if they're so smart, how come they didn't know that the right wine will make your food taste better, and the right food can make your wine taste better?

The problem is that there is no trick to matching one's food and wine, no secret formula and no hidden pathway. It is merely a matter of taste and experience, not unlike other forms of matchmaking.

You have two ways to go: you can put two likes together, or you can put two opposites together, some-times with devastating effect.

It's the peculiar, cut-grass asparagus tone that makes sauvignon blanc work with asparagus dishes. The pep-pery undercurrent of shiraz makes it a natural with steak au poivre or game, while the rich deep flavour of cabernet is made for rich gravies and meat sauces.

But put a sweet and syrupy port with a salty, aged, vein-riddled Stilton or combine the honey sweetness of a Sauternes with a lush, rich, gamey terrine and stand back and watch the fireworks. On one memorable Christmas Day I teamed a sparkling shiraz (an Australian peculi-arity) with roasted lobster, and had the time of my life.

As with most things in life, the first thing to do is to learn the rules, and the second thing is to forget them. (Drinking a lot of different wines is a sure-fire way of making sure this comes about.)

It's absolute rubbish, for example, that Chinese food can only be matched with rieslings and gewürztraminer.

Whoever came up with that one is someone who only orders ghastly Chinese-Anglo dishes like sweet-and-sour pork. One of the Great Moments In Dining is that first mouthful of smooth Burgundy after a bite of crisp-skinned, pancake-wrapped Peking duck.

The main thing is to find out what works for you. Don't, whatever you do, consult an expert. They are completely confused by the matter. While most earnest oenophiles will agree that combinations such as Brie and Burgundy, Manchego and Rioja, Münster and gewürz-traminer and Parmigiano and Barolo rank among the world's most perfect flavour marriages, wine personage Hugh Johnson is not at all convinced.

'It is a matter of faith among the wine lovers that cheese is the perfect accompaniment to any wine,' he once wrote. 'I am a dissenter to that view. All except the milder cheeses, I find, have too strong a flavour for any except the strongest tasting red wines.'

And while Chateau d'Yquem and foie gras make such a tempestuous rich-bitch-meets-spoilt-brat match that the French are thinking of pirating videos of the two together, no less an authority than the Comte de Lur Saluces whispered to me that he preferred his own Yquem with caviar. Weirdo.

Purists and readers of *The Spectator* may refuse to believe that anything less than a thirty-year-old Bordeaux is permissible with game, but I once shared a lunch with Henri Krug in Reims at which he successfully paired a bottle of his rosé Champagne with venison.

So far I've found five perfect matches in my life.

(1) Roast Cantonese duck with Domaine de la Romanée-Conti Echézeaux.

(2) A lightly poached peach with Chateau d'Yquem.

(3) Seared kangaroo and baby beetroot with Rockford Basket Press Shiraz from Australia's Barossa Valley.

(4) *Pappardelle con la lepre* (thick ribbon pasta with hare sauce) with Biondi-Santi Brunello di Montalcino.

(5) *Choucroute garni* with Trimbach Hunawihr Riesling Clos Ste-Hune.

The point is, you don't have to be a nuclear physicist to have a good time matching food and wine. In fact, it rather helps if you're not.

Starry, starry night

No, we couldn't go straight to our table. We had to go and perch on an awkwardly low ottoman in a crowded salon and drink a Champagne cocktail that had so much fruit liqueur it was impossible to tell if the Champagne were vintage or not. It was difficult to tell if it were Champagne or not.

Later, when the sniffy waiter lifted up the gleaming silver cloches only to discover that he had served the dishes to the wrong people, he got even sniffier. It was our fault, apparently, for the mix-up, for the boring serfdom of his life, for the problems with his girlfriend, for his lack of height.

When the cheese trolley rolled up, my wife asked in a whisper—everybody talked in whispers—for a little chèvre. He pointed a white-gloved finger accusingly at a little chabichou, hissing the word 'chèvre' as he did so.

Then he punched little holes in the air with his finger

"Ducasse still has a lot to learn about running a three-star restaurant. How are we supposed to respect a restaurant, and feel happy to pay its exorbitant prices, if we are made to feel at home?"

all around the cheese trolley, his voice rising with every poke. 'Chèvre, chèvre, chèvre, chèvre, chèvre, chèvre, chèvre, chèvre, chèvre, chèvre.'

Ah, the joys of eating in a French three-star restaurant in the 1980s. No wonder we soon got over it, and went back to the honest bistro and the bustling brasserie.

It was years before I was tempted back into the hallowed halls of a three-star French restaurant, curious to experience for myself the cooking of Alain Ducasse. At the turn of the century, Ducasse was the only French chef to have six stars in the *Guide Michelin* — three for his glamorous Le Louis XV restaurant in Monaco, and three for Restaurant Alain Ducasse in Paris — keeping him busy commuting weekly between the two.

But Ducasse still has a lot to learn about running a three-star restaurant. For a start, the greeting is far too friendly. How are we supposed to respect a restaurant, and feel happy to pay its exorbitant prices, if we are made to feel at home? The staff go too far out of their way to pander to their diners — to the point of providing matching little stools next to one's chair for one's handbag or briefcase. They are tall, young, attractive and speak better English than I do.

As for the wine waiter, does he really think he is doing good business to gently persuade me away from my choice of wine towards one that is a good fifty francs cheaper, and that tastes as if sent down from heaven? I'm in Paris, for goodness sake. It's my inalienable right to be ripped off, cheated, short-changed and patronised.

You can tell the place isn't working. It may be totally full, but there are far too many young French people. From memory, a proper three-star is filled with either very quiet Japanese or very loud Americans.

As for the food, where is the rich butter, cream and cognac? Why do I not feel slightly queasy after three spoonfuls? Ducasse turns to olive oil instead of butter, and Mediterranean vegetables instead of truffles and foie gras. It means this is the sort of food you can eat once or twice a week, instead of once a year. What's the point of that?

Nor does he bother to paint pretty patterns with the sauces, or attempt convoluted artistic arrangements. An entrée of cannelloni with truffled lobster, sweetbreads, cocks' combs and cocks' kidneys looks a right mess, actually, but tastes absolutely wonderful. A delicate, pot-roasted Bresse chicken with lemon, capsicum and olives is carved at the table, the way Mum does Sunday roast.

The only area in which I can see that Ducasse is true three-star status is the décor—and this is his Hotel du Parc establishment I am talking about, not the new Alain Ducasse au Plaza Athénée to which he moved in late 2000. It's appalling. The carpet is busier than L.A. International Airport, the chairs are doing something else again, and the wood panelling is very Ralph Lauren does English Club. The books in the *trompe l'oeil* library are painted with such detail it would surely have been easier to buy real volumes.

But all these complaints are ameliorated by a single,

small but charming gesture. As you leave the restaurant after your meal, you are given a large, still-warm loaf of freshly baked bread from the kitchen.

No three-star restaurant in my experience — Robuchon, Chapel, Guerard, Boyer, Bocuse, Verge, et cetera — has ever made a small but charming gesture. I would be very, very, careful if I were Alain Ducasse. The French won't put up with this for long.

"Children love black food. Anything black and sweet that is guaranteed to dye one's lips a ghastly colour and make Mum cross has got to be good."

■ Paint it black

I t's pretty obvious why I always wear black. No, I am not a man of the cloth. Nor am I a gangster, a sadist, an undertaker, a nightclub bouncer or a malcontent young rebel. Of course, it could be because I'm a wanker, but instead I prefer to say just two words that will explain everything. Squid ink.

If you have ever wrestled with a squid in the kitchen sink, pulling out its gooey innards and accidentally puncturing its ink sac, then you will know what I mean. And if you try to use those neat little sachets of Spanish squid ink instead — yes, well, been there, done that, splat, splat, splat. Either way, the kitchen is dappled in the attractive shades of fresh, hot bitumen. So is your T-shirt.

You don't want to appear at the table looking as if you have just been mud-wrestling with King Neptune, so it's off for a quick change and a big scrub before dinner. Unless, of course, you're wearing black.

Dinner itself can be a bit of a trial, too, especially if it's a nice big bowl of Spanish *arroz negro*, each grain of rice coated in swampy black ink. Or *sepia in tecia col nero*, squid cooked in a stew of its own ink. Or *spaghettini neri*, the droplets of inky sauce doing a Jackson Pollock over your shirt. Unless you're wearing black.

One false move with the breakfast crossword while eating your favourite dense, dark, sticky Swiss black cherry jam on toast, and ker-splodge. You can't go to work like that. Unless you're wearing black.

You may then find yourself dabbling with a little pitch-black olive tapenade inside your toasted focaccia at lunchtime, when naturally enough, a little dribbles onto your tie. Before you know it, you have to do embarrassing things with soda water and table napkins. Unless you're wearing black.

I simply find it easier just to buy black shirts, suits, T-shirts, ties, pants, socks and shoes. Along the way, I have become somewhat addicted to the flavour of black. Squid ink, for instance, actually tastes black. It has a sweet, scary, alien, indirect flavour lost in murky shadows, bogged down in the squishy depths of mermaids' caves.

In the same way, there is something deliciously sinister about the black velvetiness of a glass of Guinness. I love prunes, their glossy blue-black skins like black corpses. And yes, I'm the person who gets to the bag first and nicks all the black jelly beans. I love fresh licorice sticks too, huddled like illegal weapons in a paper bag.

Children love black food. Anything black and sweet

that is guaranteed to dye one's lips a ghastly colour and make Mum cross has got to be good.

For grown-ups, black truffles have a power that seems to come from the darkest and deepest of places. It is as if we have dug up part of ourselves—rotting, decomposed—from the damp soil. With voodoo-like force, they permeate the food around them until everything reeks of their brilliance. Even our hair. A truffle placed in a jar of eggs will waste no time invading the shell. Once broken, the egg will look the same, but it will taste and smell, well, black.

There is even a Chinese silky chicken with skin and flesh that is a deep tone of blue-black. No pretty dimpled blondness, no golden Sunday roasted skin, and no pale breast meat for the kiddies, just a forkful of dark, brooding flesh, and the little kiddies running screaming from the room.

Caviar was born to be black. Compare the warm, sunny, amiable orange of salmon caviar, and the happy go lucky gee-whiz sparkliness of Japanese flying fish roe to the real thing: the soft black pearls of Beluga, the dazzling ash-grey of Oscietra and the devilish glint of pitch-black Sevruga.

It must be the devil's work for an egg—that symbol of birth and purity—to be black. It's a perversion of the known and the natural, like a woman sashaying down the aisle in slinky black wedding dress and matte black lipstick. There's no way you could possibly survive such a union. Unless, of course, you're wearing black.

"The final picture of the step-by-step recipe was obviously missing. There should really have been one of Jacques Pepin collapsed, exhausted, amidst a pile of empty ice-cube trays."

Custard's last stand

There are some things that you cook, you eat, and that's it, it's all over. No great lessons are learned, not one of life's mysteries is revealed, and there is no sense of having done anything more meaningful than simply quell hunger for a few more hours.

Then there are dishes that give and give, and keep on giving. The very act of cooking them enriches your understanding of the hows and whys of the kitchen, rewarding you with small but valuable lessons that can be used time and again.

Usually, these are the edgy things, the recipes that could go horribly wrong if you are inattentive or careless, such as whipping up a soufflé or caramelising sugar.

It's that sense of living dangerously that makes success even more delicious. You know that if you rush it, or turn the heat too high or too low, or stop stirring for a second, all will be lost.

The ultimate recipe, then, is custard.

The facts are that custard is nothing more than very moist, tender gels of egg protein, and that runny custard is merely the result of continual stirring, which prevents the proteins from bonding into a fully solid mass. But, as with so much in life, the facts tell you nothing.

Custard in any of its many forms is the beauty queen of the food planet: silken, pure and fresh-tasting, with innate sensuality, a disguised richness, and an ability to empathise with young, old, rich, poor, sick and well.

To make a light, golden, runny custard is to know triumph over adversity. The first time I attempted a custard, I ended up making scrambled eggs. There is nothing remarkable about this. The first time anyone attempts a custard, they end up making scrambled eggs.

It would be easier if those who wrote recipes just wrote in the recipe: 'First, make scrambled eggs over too high a heat. Now, throw them out, lower the heat, and make a proper custard.'

My first successful runny custard was a *crème Anglaise* (French for runny custard) from page 333 of Jacques Pepin's ground-breaking book, *La Technique*. The great thing about this book was its clear, precise, step-by-step pictures. There was one showing the perfect ribbon of whisked egg yolk and sugar folding back on itself. Thrillingly, my ribbon looked exactly the same. Then, after the hot milk had been stirred in, there was a shot of Pepin's finger drawing a clear path on the back of the stirring spoon. 'The mixture should not run back together immediately; the mark should remain for a few seconds,' he explained.

I tried it and remained confused. The mark half closed but not completely. Was it ready? Do I wait? Would it be scrambled eggs again? I took a leap of faith, added a dash of cold milk to lower the temperature, and strained the lot into a chilled bowl sitting in a larger bowl filled with ice cubes. I waited for the scrambling. There was none. It was perfect.

The only trouble was, I was a wreck. The final picture of the step-by-step was obviously missing. There should really have been one of Pepin collapsed, exhausted, amidst a pile of empty ice-cube trays.

It may have been nerve-racking, but I learned an important truth. You can't hurry custard. Making it is one of the great slowing-down moments of your life, like throwing a line into a river and waiting for a bite, or letting a kid fall asleep on your lap.

Once you've failed scrambled eggs and passed on custard, it's time to specialise. Firm custards, such as baked custard tart, rice custard, the much-maligned quiche, and the purest and prettiest steamed custard of them all, the Japanese *chawan mushi*, are all far less scary to make.

Mack Sennett and his slapstick pals weren't as silly as they thought they were. They knew that a baked custard is a wondrous, magical thing, and that the true nature of comedy is to take what is sublime and revered, and then hurl it in your face. I'd love to see what they would have done with crème anglaise.

"The moral of the story: never trust a person who won't wash the dishes with you. It means they don't want to talk to you, or get to know you any better. They are rejecting you."

All washed up

I like to wash. I like the fresh lemony smell of the detergent, the steam of the hot water, the clatter and clunk of good crockery in the sink. Sometimes I get more of a sense of achievement from doing the dishes than I did cooking the meal. See that shine? I did that. See those stacks of gleaming plates, and rows of glasses? Me.

It is one of the few miracles not in the Bible, as the crusted and the dirty become clear and sparkling; and the besmirched and smeared are restored to their natural state.

Doing the dishes is an act of restoration, and of transformation. It is one of the most positive things we can do in our day. It is giving thanks—for our food, which we can relive as we wash off the remnants, and for our worldly goods, which we are washing. There is almost instant gratification in changing a room that looks as if Godzilla has just dropped in for lunch to a room that makes you want to cook something. Gosh, I had no idea I had a marble bench under all that—how nice.

Even the zoomiest rice cooker will take twenty minutes before you can appreciate the end result. For a cake, it's an hour. For a duck confit, it's a matter of weeks. But with the washing up, it's slosh slosh, rub rub, wipe wipe and it's done.

We all like to think that the table is the pivotal centre of the family, the thing that draws us together, but the real stuff tends to happen later, after the table has broken up. It's as if there is a camera, so everyone acts up for it. Then you take the camera away and they relax. That's what happens at the sink.

Conveniently, the world is divided into those who wash, and those who dry. The washers are the doers, the sleeve-roller-uppers who don't mind getting their hands dirty—or clean. They are task-oriented people who know they have to put their backs into something if they want their life to work.

Dryers, on the other hand, are the finessers, the stylists, the philosophers of the kitchen, with a theory on everything. All have their own formula for how long to leave the dishes in a rack, when to use a fresh towel, or whether to put away as they go, or stack, then store. They like to admire things as they go, arrange them neatly on the shelf, and pause occasionally to enjoy their handiwork.

In the meantime, the washers and the dryers are talking, bonding over the bubbles. I have seen my father-in-law (a dryer) go through an entire dinner party without saying a word to my brother-in-law's wife (a washer). Yet once dinner is over, they like to retire, not for port, but for detergent and rubber gloves, where they stand side by side telling yarns like two old buddies at a regiment reunion.

And yet, I am suspicious of people who feel the need to race out of their dining chairs the second the coffee is drained. Washing up is not meant to break into the communion of the table, but to be a sequel to it. Nor am I fond of those who keep putting it off, as if the dishes will wash themselves, thus robbing the meal of its natural ending.

Which brings me to the moral of the story: never trust people who won't wash the dishes with you. It means they don't want to talk to you, or get to know you any better. They are rejecting you. The hostess who insists you don't enter her kitchen, the boyfriend who refuses to let you pick up the rubber gloves, the sister who sneaks out and does the dishes all by herself when you're not looking . . . these people have hot and cold running emotional problems.

We need a new term to describe the act of doing the dishes, one that suggests pleasure and praise instead of duty and detergent.

Then we could just pop off for some post-nourishment cleansing and dehydration in the cookware centre wellness day spa, and have the time of our lives.